BECOMING A FEARLESS
YOUNG ARTIST

Becoming A Fearless Young Artist

LaQuet Sharnell Pringle

Contents

Resource Link and Code

For access to the templates & videos within this book, visit the link below:

www.fyastudios.co/fearless-book-extras

password: iamfearless

Dedication

I dedicate this book to everyone who
dreams of stepping onto a stage, but is still
uncertain about where to turn.
You are on the right path when you are
Bold, Brave, Playful, and Fearless!

To my kiddo, a daily inspiration to go
further and play more freely.

To my wife, the greatest
Love I've ever known.
Because of you, I can.

A Fearless Manifesto

We will be bold, brave, playful, and fearless.
The world needs our voices and stories to break down
barriers and share joy with all humanity.

We'll be fearless by focusing on our goals and
sharpening our tools with love and passion.
We can and will create from a place of truth and
vulnerability—even when the ghost lights go down.

Because joy is meant for everyone, we will,
Be Bold. Be Brave. Be Playful.
Then we will Be Fearless.

Prologue

Have you ever stood in the wings with your heart pounding, knowing the lights are about to shine on you and the story you must tell in just a few moments?

That feeling of anticipation, fear, and excitement is part of the fiber that makes every performing artist's journey beautiful.

Waiting in the wings is a large part of what artists do in their careers. We wait to book a job, wait to be accepted into the college, wait to receive responses from grant submissions, or wait to be called into a room to audition. The trick to waiting in the wings is acknowledging how it will impact you once your opportunity comes.

In the pages of this book, we'll explore the preparation stages for waiting in the wings at the start of your career. Whether you're heading into college, moving to "The BIG City," or you're a parent searching for a better understanding of how to support your child's creativity, we will explore the beautiful ways your artistic craft can be honed with Ease, Flow, and Connectivity. You get to choose when to start your career, and over time, with the awareness of how to sharpen your skills and become the best version of yourself, your artistry will shine brighter and more fearlessly.

The performing arts ask and often demand that artists show up to work with vulnerability, perseverance, and passion. Mr. Shakespeare said it best: "To thine own self be true." The truth of knowing, expressing, identifying, and investing in yourself will clear a runway to being more vulnerable in your work, persevering through tough times, and always performing with a fiery passion.

Owning this truth is what defines a **Fearless Young Artist**.

I've dedicated my life to the craft of performing, creating, and educating young, emerging, and professional artists through Fearless Young Artists Studios. The arts provide me with the air to fill my lungs every morning as I seek new ways to create opportunities for myself professionally and personally. I'm an artist because creativity is how I navigate life's many storms. Having learned to be a *fearless* artist grounds and humbles me. It allows me to welcome and enjoy the highs and lows of living my daily life to the fullest.

This perspective on fearlessness came later in my life and career. I was newly married when I first asked myself, "How much can I give to my creativity, and how much can my creativity give to me?" This question led me away from the stage and toward an existential sabbatical from performing on Broadway.

I wanted more time. I wanted the time to address aspects of myself I was afraid of, to set new goals, to live a life beyond an eight-show, six-day-a-week work schedule, and to gain an appreciation for my body, something for which I'd only scratched the surface.

Because I took the time I needed, I found myself in an observational mode after a two-year hiatus from my professional performing career. I identified problems and solutions that helped me find ease, flow, and a sense of connectivity with myself. Before my break, I would become crippled with anxiety, insecurity, and depression while trying to perform on Broadway, prepare myself for auditions, and develop the relationships required to expand my career further.

Thankfully, I listened and arrived at a place of greater accessibility within my craft as an artist, coach, and educator, marking the most fearless chapter of my life.

I am writing about the journey I wish had been shared with *myself* when I began the long trek of creating a life filled with artistry in every step I took.

Thus far, my journey has been 21 years in the commercial musical theater (Broadway: *Mrs. Doubtfire, Memphis, Sweet Charity, The Lion King, Lysistrata Jones*), TV/Film (*The Daily Show, I.F., Blacklist, Girls on the Bus*), VoiceOvers (Geico), and Commercials and Regional Theater (too many to list). As an educator and coach, the past 12 years have taken me to multiple universities, colleges, and conservatories, including Texas State, PACE University, AMDA, Texas Christian University, the New York Film Academy, and countless dance and theater studios across North America.

As the owner and founder of Fearless Young Artists Studios, based in Harlem, I've found myself not only teaching the next generation of young artists but also developing a methodology to enhance the instruments of young, emerging, and professional performers. Time and experience have led me to hone in on how students should lead with *ease* in the application of technique, *flow* from onstage to off, and remain *connected* in the many stages an artist will experience. Artistic humans everywhere can apply this mind-body connection to utilize their body's ability to express themselves in healthy and creative ways. As an artist who lived through many years of toxic work environments, unhealthy relationships with food and my body, and constant over-analyzation of things that were out of my control, my methodology (**The Onset Technique**) is a love sonnet to creating a legacy of safe artistic practices for my people: performing artists.

Please don't expect to finish this and immediately book your first Broadway show. If it happens, CALL ME IMMEDIATELY AND GOOD FOR YOU, FRIEND! But truthfully, the road to outward success can and will take time. When it became clear that I needed to step away from the stage, I incorporated this technique into every aspect of my creative life. This work requires introspection, self-awareness, and the ability to surrender to the process of living a creative life.

The truth is, the business of show is an incredibly arduous one. However, being an artist is where we find the melody of life.

A part of our brain experiences a Dopamine release when we learn, create, explore, and develop new things. When we come into a rehearsal studio and learn new music, lines, or choreography, Dopamine is released, and our brains repeatedly want to feel that "high." Being creative is AWESOME! And yet, even the best roller coaster rides come to a stop and require you to stand in line all over again if you wish to ride again.

Life is A Thing, but it's a Whole Awesome Thing when you lead a *creative* life.

The "high" feeling isn't solely related to performing, booking, or getting into *that* college. It's also within the community that surrounds you. From photographers, theater companies, unions, and classes in your neighborhoods, you are surrounded by like-minded and like-bodied people seeking to create and to do so with you!

You are more than capable of achieving everything you seek in life. With these practical, holistic, and community-based tools, you'll find the inspiration needed to begin your journey into the performing arts. If you're afraid or nervous, maybe even now as you hold this book, know that you've already done one of the hardest things an artist can do: acknowledging that fear and proceeding anyway.

I am so proud of you.

We are embarking on a long journey ahead, so let's step into it by reciting these words daily:

I'm being Bold, Brave, and Playful. I'm Being Fearless!

At 19, I began my career in commercial musical theater. I spent a year at the University of North Carolina School of the Arts, and every day there, I knew I was developing skills that would translate to a career onstage, particularly one that would define who I wanted to become as an artist in the entertainment industry.

In my first year of college, I took it upon myself to begin developing the skills of building an audition songbook, learning how to handle open chorus calls, finding an agent, approaching acting sides, and creating my look (now known as brand building). I learned the basic tools from summer intensives and workshops in high school, so much of this information gathering was familiar. I thought everyone had these tools. I thought I needed to "catch up". I quickly learned this was untrue. Most people around me didn't know how to do any of these things. This book was essentially born there.

A decade into my professional performing career, I found purpose in beginning my journey as an educator, coach, and mentor. The pandemic opened my eyes to even more ways to explore my life as a choreographer, director, writer, and creative entrepreneur that I am today. I also knew it was time to write.

You have the fortitude to be a **Fearless Young Artist** because you were inspired enough to open a book called *Becoming the Fearless Young Artist*. You may be a parent who wants only the best for your child. I understand the desire to ensure your child has a well-planned career path in a field that is largely unpredictable. I want the same for my child. I also understand what it was like to be on the verge of choosing, attending, and ultimately graduating from college with a pocket full of dreams and sunshine, along with questions about those "best-case scenario" situations my college put me in. Most compassionately, I understand and empathize with professionals working in their field, but feel that "There's Gotta Be Something Better Than This."

As you navigate these pages, I hope you understand this is just the beginning. These pages are a place to enhance the questions you'll inevitably have for your coaches, teachers, and community. When in doubt, know that you are moving closer to becoming fearless, indirectly and directly empowering those around you. Your peers will see in you what it looks like to stare down a challenge and do every-thing possible to conquer it.

My fearless friend, you never know who you're inspiring, so keep up the good work of transforming yourself. Your community will follow your bold, brave, play-ful, and fearless approach.

Inside these pages, you will find resume templates, advice on auditions, journal prompts, and an introduction to The Onset Technique, which will develop your voice, movement, and imaginary world as an actor. All of this is necessary to under-stand the introductory history of Broadway, where the industry is headed next, and how your unique voice is needed to contribute to commercial theater.

Let's dive in and get you one step closer to finding your fearless artistry in a way that brings ease, flow, and connectivity to your process in the performing arts.

I'll see you in Chapter 1 of class.

1

Why Are You Passionate?

When you first felt the pull toward the stage, I imagine the fun of pretending most engaged you. Perhaps you enjoyed creating original works around your home or community and found a sense of expression and freedom in that imaginary world.

Moments like these inspire many performing artists, particularly those passionate about theater. I want us to begin by answering a few key questions:

- Describe the last time you were onstage.
- When, onstage, do you lose yourself in an imaginary world?
- What does storytelling mean to you?
- In how many ways do you aspire to tell stories?

The answers to these questions define why you aspire to perform on Broadway. As Simon Sinek teaches us, knowing our "Why" draws loyal customers (potential employers) to our business (our work as artists).

And you are a business.

You are in the business of performing works from diverse artists eight times a week, often with no "off" season and limited time to recover before performing onstage again. Therefore, it is crucial to understand why you want to pursue a career with its fair and unfair share of ups and downs. Equally crucial is knowing how to navigate those ups and downs.

Once you know your "why," we can nurture a fearless entrepreneurial spirit, a youthful approach to engaging with the arts, and a mindset that allows you to interpret others' works and create original pieces to express and share your voice unapologetically.

"Broadway" is the stretch of midtown in New York City where shows are performed in theaters that begin at 66th Street and Broadway and run down to 40th Street between 8th Avenue to 6th Avenue.

<u>There are about 41 professional theaters, each with a seating capacity of 583 or more.</u>

If you're a theatre fan, you can see anything on Broadway, from new musicals and plays to concerts and variety shows. Because the theater district offers a wide range of entertainment for its audiences, it is known for its high production values, talented casts, and compelling storytelling.

For many, Broadway represents the highest standards in the performing arts. As a 21-year veteran of performing on and off Broadway, training to perform on Broadway can be compared to that of an Olympic athlete whose sport spans an entire calendar year.

Who has Ownership of Broadway Theaters?

Broadway theaters in New York City are primarily owned and operated by three major organizations: The Shubert Organization, The Nederlander Organization, and Jujamcyn Theaters.

- <u>The Shubert Organization</u> is the largest and most influential theater owner on Broadway, owning and operating 17 theaters across the city. Established in the early 1900s by the Shubert brothers — Sam, Lee, and Jacob J. Shubert — this organization has significantly shaped the Broadway landscape as it is known today. (Shows performed here include: *Chicago, Othello* with Denzel Washington & Jake Gyllenhaal, *John Proctor is the Villain*)

- The Nederlander Organization owns and operates nine theaters on Broadway. Founded in 1912, this family-run company has been a key player in the Broadway industry, producing and presenting numerous iconic shows. (Shows performed here include: *The Color Purple, Hello Dolly, Kimberly Akimbo*)
- Jujamcyn Theaters owns and operates five Broadway theaters. Founded in the mid-20th century, the company is known for nurturing creative, high-profile productions and often taking risks on groundbreaking new works. (Shows performed here include: *Hadestown, Sunset Blvd* with Nicole Scherzinger, *The Book of Mormon, Moulin Rouge*)

Lincoln Center also owns a Broadway theater — the Vivian Beaumont Theater. This cultural epicenter (New York City Opera, New York City Ballet, American Ballet Theater, and the NYC Metropolitan Opera) adds a not-for-profit presence to the Broadway landscape.

There are also a few independently owned houses, such as the Hayes Theater (owned by Second Stage Theater), the Circle in the Square Theatre — the only theater in the round on Broadway, the Hudson Theatre, and the Lyric Theatre. These independent owners contribute to the much-needed variety of productions seen on Broadway while also bringing a level of diversity within the Broadway lens.

Who is The Broadway League?

The Broadway League is the national trade association for the Broadway industry, representing theater owners, producers, presenters, general managers, and various other professionals involved in producing Broadway shows. In layman's terms, the Broadway League is the producers' and theater owners' union. *(More on unions in Chapter 4.)*

Founded in 1930 as the "League of New York Theatres and Producers," the Broadway League addressed industry-related issues, including labor relations, marketing, and public relations.

Over time, it has expanded its influence to include touring productions and is a major player in the national and international theater scene.

How the Broadway League's History Affects Aspiring Performing Artists

The Broadway League's history and role in the industry are to promote Broadway and touring productions, therefore shaping the environment in which performers work. The League's initiatives (including the Tony Awards and The Jimmy Awards, educational outreach programs, and industry conferences) provide artists with opportunities for exposure, networking, and professional development.

Knowing about the theaters, their owners, and those who'll help produce the work you bring to the stage will enhance you as a creative entrepreneur who utilizes their talent to navigate the business of show.

As we move forward, begin asking yourself:

- In what theater is your favorite show currently being performed?
- Who owns that theater?
- Do the creative teams or producers of your favorite shows frequently rent space from the same theater owners?
- Do you want your work performed in one of the primary Broadway theaters or an independent theater?

- If you "just want to book a show," is your talent diversified enough to lend itself to the spaces available on Broadway?

Who Owns Off-Broadway Theaters?

Off-Broadway theaters in New York City are typically owned by various entities, including non-profit theater companies. Examples of non-profit organizations that produce Off-Broadway theater include:

- The Public Theater known for producing works like *Hamilton* or *Hell's Kitchen* before they moved to Broadway.
- Roundabout Theatre Company is a major non-profit that operates both Broadway and Off-Broadway spaces. The Roundabout Theater is where *Pirates! The Penzance Musical* was recently staged.
- Signature Theatre focuses on honoring the work of specific playwrights. Sarah Ruhl's *Eurydice* was performed there, but other notable writers' works have received residency through the Signature Theater, such as Dominique Morisseau and Samuel D. Hunter.

Additionally, numerous independent producers create their work in Off-Broadway theaters, and these individuals often lease spaces for various productions.

My favorites are the educational institutions, home to many Off-Broadway theaters and shows. Many of these theaters are owned by universities or colleges with thriving performing arts programs, such as NYU's Skirball Center for the Performing Arts.

Private investors or collectives are theaters owned by private investors or groups of artists who come together to create spaces for innovative work. Collectives and organizations such as The Pit, Upright Citizens Brigade, WP Theater, Transport Group, and Freestyle Love Supreme.

Benefits for Performers Working Off-Broadway

Artistic freedom and innovation are the cornerstones of Off-Broadway productions. Often, Off-Broadway offers more creative freedom than Broadway. Performers and creators can take more risks, explore experimental works, and engage in more avant-garde storytelling, where thought-provoking and inspirational ideas can emerge.

This is accomplished first and foremost because the theaters are generally smaller and more intimate. <u>Off-Broadway theaters have 100 to 499 seats.</u>

Off-Broadway is a home for diversity. Performers can explore and create fearlessly in various characters and genres, which can be valuable for your artistic development and career growth.

In these smaller theaters, many performers build careers and distinguish their work as a stepping stone to larger opportunities, including Broadway, television, film, and community engagement.

Off-Broadway is a respected platform where emerging artists can flourish because of the connectivity between life and art.

The Daily Practice of Finding Balance

Speaking of connecting life and art, the concept of the "work-life" balance seems to ring louder when you leave for college, are just graduating, are in some kind of personal or professional transition, or are perhaps experiencing a breakthrough. At every stage of your life, you'll be practicing finding balance.

Like many other people in various fields, many performing artists struggle with this as well. This is primarily due to scheduling conflicts, limited funding, and the demanding nature of living in a city like New York City. Often, Off-Broadway schedules can be less demanding than Broadway schedules. Not always, but occasionally. This provides performers with a better daily practice of finding balance, enabling you, the artist, to pursue other creative or personal commitments, secure work that generates additional income, and allow your body to recover properly.

The Off-Broadway scene is best known for its close-knit community. It's a place where creative artists support one another and build camaraderie, which is beneficial for networking, finding collaborators, and establishing long-term professional relationships. This provides an essential foundation within the New York theater scene.

Now that you have an introduction to some history of the commercial theaters in NYC and where performing artists can perform and produce their work, grab your notebooks! I'll see you in Chapter 2 to create some realistic and practical goals.

2

Build Your Skills

The challenges and demands of a Broadway career are not for the faint of heart. The grueling schedule can be stressful for the artists' bodies, minds, and spirits.

When I met my wife, we had date nights on Monday evenings or after my shows, which meant the date began at 11 p.m. We maintained that schedule as we built our connection with one another over five years. My craft flourished as I found new ways to sharpen my instrument; however, my personal life took a back seat. I share this with you because we will discuss how to train, recover, and live your best life! This will allow our bodies more access to ease in developing new skills to support your personal and professional growth.

The key ingredient to any successful career is exemplary training and education. Choosing the best college, university, or conservatory is the best decision you can make in beginning your career. I have graduated from a conservatory (William Esper Studios), attended a university/conservatory (University of North Carolina School of the Arts), and finally graduated from a state college (SUNY Empire State University - BA - Magna Cum Laude). Additionally, I've taught within these types of programs, so I am more than capable of helping you navigate each option.

Conservatory

Enrolling in a two-year conservatory program offers intensive training that hones an artist's craft and prepares them for the demands of a professional career. Over two years, artists engage in rigorous daily practice, receive personalized instruction from industry professionals, and participate in numerous showcases and performances. For parents, a two-year conservatory program offers the assurance that their child is receiving a well-rounded artistic education, which includes both practical training and the development of critical thinking skills, providing a strong foundation for either direct entry into the industry or further academic pursuits.

On the other hand, a one-year conservatory program is ideal for young artists eager to fast-track their careers while gaining concentrated, high-quality training. In just one year, students are immersed in an intensive environment that emphasizes hands-on experience and immediate application of skills, making it a powerful option for those who are focused and ready to enter the professional world.

Of these two options, I strongly advocate for the two-year conservatory. And you may be saying, "But, LaQuet! I'm ready to perform now! I don't want to wait two years!" If you want to be a performing artist, two years of investing in yourself and your craft is a drop in the bucket over a lifetime.

BFA - Four-Year Conservatory Colleges & Universities

Pursuing a four-year college or university degree in the arts offers young artists a structured environment to hone their craft, receive a comprehensive education, and graduate with a degree, ultimately maturing with focus into adulthood. These programs provide access to experienced faculty, state-of-the-art facilities, and a supportive community of like-minded peers.

Students benefit from a well-rounded curriculum that includes practical training in their chosen discipline and academic courses that broaden their understanding of history, literature, and culture. This combination enhances their artistic abilities and equips them with critical thinking, communication, and problem-solving skills, making them more versatile and adaptable in the business of show.

For parents, investing in an artistic degree program can offer peace of mind if you feel confident in the department and its leaders' ability to provide a high-quality artistic education to prepare your child for various career paths within and beyond the arts. Colleges and universities often have strong alumni networks and connections with industry professionals, providing students with valuable internships, mentorships, and post-graduate employment opportunities.

Additionally, the degree serves as a credential that can open doors to teaching, graduate studies, or other professional opportunities. A four-year degree nurtures a young artist's passion. It lays a solid foundation for a sustainable and fulfilling career if you're solely interested in performing the works of others or helping other artists bring their creative works to the stage.

BA - Four-Year Liberal Arts Colleges & Universities

Pursuing a four-year liberal arts degree at a college or university provides young artists with a well-rounded education beyond training solely within the performing arts. These programs equip student artists with the critical thinking, writing, public speaking, and problem-solving skills necessary to thrive in the ever-evolving world of the arts and communication.

While a conservatory BFA focuses intensively on craft, a liberal arts education broadens an artist's perspective by integrating courses from the humanities, social sciences, and natural sciences.

This multidisciplinary approach fosters intellectual curiosity and creativity, encouraging students to draw connections between their art and the world around them.

Additionally, at a liberal arts college or university, students will dive into the historical context of the arts. They will critically analyze themes and practices that could encourage innovative thoughts and creative works as they develop their artistic voice.

As a graduate of a liberal arts program, this training enhanced my professional experience and helped inspire the work I create today.

When I returned to college to complete my degree after leaving the University of North Carolina School of the Arts, I was 16 years into my professional performing career. My academic advisor asked me, "What did you learn from performing that you'd like to reinvestigate or challenge?"

If she asked me that today, I'd say, "I want to orchestrate the symphony of experiences that have led to this time in space through education, writing, choreography, and direction. I want *all* uplifting and inspiring voices and stories to come forward, not just a chosen few."

In every piece I work on, I think of this question. My need to create answers for the world surrounding my community and myself is reflected in how I build my imaginary worlds as a writer, choreographer, director, and educator.

Your (or your child's) pursuit of a liberal arts degree can reassure them that they are developing their artistic talents and gaining a versatile education that will open doors to various career paths within and beyond the arts. Graduates from liberal arts programs are well-prepared for the unpredictable nature of the arts, as this holistic education ensures that young artists are not only equipped to excel in their chosen craft but also empowered to lead fulfilling, multi-faceted lives.

These options are crucial during the early stages of an artist's training. If your goal is to be onstage, then diversifying your talent is the next major topic for a performing artist.

There is a common misconception that to be on Broadway, you must sing, act, *and* dance. While this can be true, it is not the rule to live by. What's missing here is space for actors who write, singers who are composers and songwriters, dancers who are choreographers/directors, and, of course, performing artists who can produce excellent shows. I want to explore how being a multi-hyphenate can and should be developed based on your interests. These insights can cross-train your mindset as a performing artist while continually inspiring yourself.

Singer/Actors = Leading roles

An actor or singer in a leading role is more than just the face of the show; they are highly skilled artists who analyze a script and guide the audience through the story. Actors such as Rob McClure, Audra McDonald, and Brandon Victor Dixon are just a few artists who inspire us to train with the eye of a director who seeks to connect the story from beginning to end. Artists like these are thoughtful, exploratory, and detail-oriented. They understand the script so well they can move seamlessly from song to scene, just as a bird takes flight. How? Because they trained with a director's hawk eye.

How do I train with a director's hawk eye?

READ EVERYTHING! Read scripts, screenplays, newspapers, blogs, books, novels, social media captions, and SIGNS! Your imagination and insight into language will bring pictures to life for the characters you create. Also, read everything multiple times and in various places and spaces.

When watching a show on stage, don't only think about what you like about it, but also about what you didn't like, how you might approach the character, *and why*. When you have a WHY, you have a sense of self and freedom when performing or preparing for the stage.

Ask yourself consistently how you feel about the words in the works you're studying or performing. This is the foundation of your point of view.

Try this exercise today: film yourself saying, "I Feel (insert a verb or adverb) about this *(insert a noun)...*"

For example, today I noticed myself saying, "I Feel encouraged about the state of the world when I see children laughing, smiling, and playing." The day before, I felt rested and eager to start a new work.

Start every sentence with this for one minute.

Now repeat and film yourself for two minutes.

Continue to increase the time until you reach five minutes.

This level of connection forms the basis for approaching various topics, obstacles, and ideas. Similar to a Meisner acting exercise, the more you repeat something, the more you experience new feelings, thoughts, and experiences while repeating the same thing continually. If, during the process of increasing the time limit, you feel the "pull," "spark," or "impulse" to change the repetition, please do. But continually start the repetition with "I Feel." A good director is highly attuned with what they are feeling, thinking, experiencing, and learning. Unlocking that superpower strength begins with knowing how you feel about everything.

An actor who performs with a director's eye can mellifluously carry an audience through an imaginary experience and then return the audience and themselves to reality after the curtain call. The "I Feel" exercise is the pathway for you to receive and give the empowerment you need to captivate an audience, ultimately establishing your Point of View.

An actor without a point of view sets themselves up for misdirection and self-doubt. Your voice is needed to grow the story, so it's wise to know yourself within the story and in connection with others, like a hawk.

Singer/Songwriters & Actors = Ensemble-Driven shows

I love artists, such as Sarah Bareilles, Lin-Manuel Miranda, Jonathan Larson, and Shaina Taub, because they bring unique experiences to their work in a way that shifts the cultural landscape of theater. The music becomes an extension of the script, meaning the actors who bring the story to life truly illuminate the notes on the page.

You may find yourself drawn to artists like Levi Kreis (Tony Award Winner - *Million Dollar Quartet*), Harry Connick Jr. (Grammy Award winner and celebrated jazz musician, Broadway actor - *Pajama Game*), Cristin Milioti (*Once, How I Met Your Mother, Wolf of Wall Street*), and for good reason. They are phenomenal examples of how a talent in one discipline can grow into another talent (also known as scaling). Artists who can play instruments, sing, and act are rare and possess unique versatility. When booked on a show, these artists bring groundedness and playfulness to their casts.

How, you may be asking? I'm willing to bet lots of money that a jam session is going down between shows at the theater or in a studio somewhere. I bet someone is freestyling (dancing, singing, rapping, etc.) on breaks. These are the artists who continually experiment with ideas and inspirations. You will be fortunate to have artists like this in your show, as they remind us that this show is for the audience, but the next creation is already cooking. That air has a tingling excitement that I have felt in many companies and shows. Shoutout to John Rua, Daniel Watts, Nick Blaimire, Calvin Cooper, and Dionne Figgins, to name a few, who I have watched and basked in the richness of their freestyles on breaks.

Dancer/Singer/Actor = The Traditional Triple Threat

I humbly am in this category, but I am not alone. Many artists, such as Afra Hines (*Dancin'*, *Hadestown*, *In the Heights*, *Hamilton*), Katy Webber (*Tina*, *Smash*, *Memphis*, *Wicked*), Aaron J. Albano (*25th Annual Putnam County Spelling Bee*, *Newsies*, *Hamilton*), or Ephriam Sykes (*Ain't Too Proud*, *Our Town*, *Memphis*, *Newsies*) are talents who can easily transition from the ensemble to a leading role with ease, grace, and sophistication. Artists who wear the Triple Threat crown often have a strong background in some form of classical dance or movement. From there, triple-threat artists find confidence to grow complex physicality into varying roles because we've trained by focusing on all three disciplines to be utilized in every show we perform.

Performing and Producing = The Innovator

Artists who perform and produce their work in commercial musical theater are true innovators. They redefine what it means to be a creator in the industry. By wearing multiple hats — writing, composing, acting, and producing — they share their vision from concept to completion on stage. Their artistic intent remains intact, allowing them to express their beliefs about themselves and our collective history within contemporary society. Once again, I find myself here frequently.

As mentioned, Sara Bareilles transitioned from a successful pop music career to writing and producing the Broadway musical *Waitress*. Her involvement in the creation and production of the show allowed her to bring a fresh, contemporary voice to Broadway, blending her pop sensibilities with traditional musical theater storytelling. (It also didn't hurt that Sara majored in Communications at UCLA — Hi, Liberal Arts undergraduate degree.)

Artists such as Stew, creator of *Passing Strange*, and Michael R. Jackson, the creator of *A Strange Loop*, have also made significant contributions to commercial theater by producing their work.

Passing Strange is a semi-autobiographical musical that blends rock, gospel, and punk music to tell a coming-of-age story that explores identity, art, and race. Stew's involvement in every aspect of the production allowed the show to retain his deeply personal and authentic voice, making it stand apart in the musical theater landscape. Stew did not attend college, instead studying at the school of life. Further proving that the world is a classroom if you are open to learning from it.

Similarly, Michael R. Jackson's *A Strange Loop*, which won the Pulitzer Prize for Drama, is an intensely personal exploration of a Black, Queer writer's struggles with self-identity. Jackson's role as the show's writer and producer allowed him to tackle complex and often underrepresented themes with unflinching honesty. He broke new ground in how stories are told on the commercial stage. Michael R. Jackson attended NYU Tisch School, earning a BFA and MFA.

Another artist to mention is Nick Blaemire. Blaemire's musical *Glory Days*, which he wrote while still in college at the University of Michigan, marked him as one of the youngest writers to have a show produced on Broadway. Although *Glory Days* had a brief run, Blaemire continued to innovate, blending his performance experience with his writing skills to create works that reflect contemporary life.

Finally, and most notably, Lin-Manuel Miranda starred in, wrote, and produced *Hamilton* and *In the Heights*. Blending hip-hop and history in the theater which has captivated Broadway and created a new genre of writing within the theater. Lin attended Wesleyan University as a double major in film and theater.

These artist-producers aren't just making content and then performing; they are driven by a desire to create work that resonates on a deeper level, both artistically and culturally. These artists are innovators because they aren't just contributing to the theater but are actively shaping its future, bringing new voices, styles, and stories to the forefront.

If you have a story within you, producing your work could challenge the status quo, open up new possibilities for what theater can be, and express your unique point of view, which is a key component of being a **Fearless Young Artist**.

As you begin your journey of training as a performing artist, keep these ideas and artists in mind when choosing a program to attend, as it will significantly shape what kind of artist you'd like to be.

The FYA Studios community provides support and collaboration to empower your choices in discovering who you are as an artist.

3

The Professional Journey: Building Your Portfolio,

F riend, every profession has must-haves. For performing artists, these include a resume, website, headshots, representation, audition opportunities, and attending networking events.

In this chapter, I'll provide templates and advice on all your must-haves.

As you follow this section, it's vital to remember that as you evolve as an artist and human, so will your professional must-haves. Everything we cover here must be updated every three to five (3-5) years or for every professional opportunity earned.

Your resume is a written glimpse into your work as an artist. It details the mediums you've performed and allows you to start a conversation when you're auditioning and meeting with representatives or schools/programs. If you don't have a resume, you'll find it much more challenging to book auditions, get representation, or advance your career, no matter your chosen field.

The key points in building a resume for a performing artist are:

First and Last Name: Listed at the top and underlined. The font size should be between 20 and 30, and Times/Times Roman or a similar font should be used.

Contact information: Listed directly below your name. The font size should be between 10 and 12, in Times New Roman or a similar font. Email, social media handles, and cell phone number are the best forms of contact to include.

Union Affiliation: If you are a union member, including this information under your name and contact details at the top center of the page is very helpful. Popular actor unions are: AEA (Actors' Equity Association), SAG/AFTRA (Screen Actors Guild - American Federation of Television and Radio Artists), AGMA (American Guild of Musical Artists), AGVA (American Guild of Variety Artists)

Stats: Your stats, such as height and vocal range, are essential for casting and creative teams to know where you'd be cast within the full show; often referred to as "Type." Additionally, Artists usually include their pronouns in this line.

I do not recommend adding weight, eye color, or hair color, as these are elements of you that can change and evolve quickly.

Credits: The standard list begins with theater, followed by TV/film, showcases, commercials, voiceovers, and concerts. However, if you start to book (land or secure work) more in TV, film, voiceover, etc., list the credits you have the most of first.

In each of these categories, list your credits in three (3) categories: Name of show, the role you performed, location, or director of show. Note that roles should be listed as Character's Name, Featured Character's Name, Ensemble, Featured Ensemble, U/S (Understudy – list all roles you understudy in a show), Swing, Principal Stand-By.

Education/Training: This category presents a prime opportunity to engage in conversations during auditions and meetings. It's best to begin by listing home training options (such as local dance, theater, or music studios), as well as high school, undergraduate, and graduate programs. Once you've graduated from a university, college, or conservatory, remove your high school and local training. If you attend a conservatory after your undergraduate studies, replace your high school and local training with the conservatory program as the second line under your undergraduate program.

After you've listed your academic study, list your masterclasses and workshops. They should be listed: voice, acting, dance, summer intensives/workshops (i.e., continuing education)

Special Skills: The best part of this category is that EVERY-THING IS A SPECIAL SKILL! Do you babysit? That's a special skill! Do you recite the alphabet backward? That's a special skill! Tumbling, roller skating, rollerblading, crocheting, sewing, technical skills, driver's licenses, passports, and languages spoken are all valuable skills.

Here is a link to templates for you to download and follow. I've included my resume and CV to show you how a seasoned veteran formats this crucial piece of professionalism. You can find it in the Resume + Reel Templates section of the book.

This simple list will ensure you are polished and ready to put your best self forward.

Reels

Over my 21 years working in commercial musical theater, an artist's reel has become a key component in building a professional portfolio. This can be challenging when performing primarily in the theater, as most theaters cannot share recordings of performances. To circumvent this, we must create as close to performance-ready footage of our work as possible for our websites, casting websites, and social media.

Many actors use a self-tape format to begin this process. The following are points that will help you film the best performance reel.

Time: It should be 2 minutes *maximum*.

Performance: Music - Two contrasting songs of 32-64 bars of an uptempo and a ballad. **Dance** - a solo of your best style, or 90-second clips of varying movement styles. **Acting** - Drop in to the meatiest part of a 1-minute monologue or short scene. The monologues should be contrasting, comedic, or dramatic.

The last element of your reel should be a clip or two of doing your best or most favorite special skill.

Point of View: The only person in the film should be YOU! We love duets and large group numbers, but in a performance reel, you want to showcase *your* best work. Focusing on only one person in your footage will engage the audience more effectively.

Sound: Your voice has to be center stage when singing and acting. Think of shows like *American Idol*, where the audition process accentuates the artist's voice, not the musical accompaniment. However, if you want to showcase that you play an instrument and sing, ensure that your instrument complements your singing and that the sound suits both the instrument and the vocal performance.

Actors, be mindful of your dynamic volume when performing your monologues or scenes. If your piece involves your voice and showcases loudness (such as yelling, passion, or intensity), ensure the levels are set to avoid damaging the audience's hearing.

If you have professional credits from TV or film, adding them to your professional reel is necessary. The most reliable source to find your footage if you've worked on major productions (major motion pictures, networks, and most streaming services) is *Reel Today. This company has swift turnarounds and affordable prices.

This company does not compensate me; I am a professional actor who has successfully used it.

Headshots

I love getting new headshots! It's a day when you become your most fantastic and fancy self. The headshot is your second professional calling card that industry professionals will use to remember you. This portrait should capture you on your best day while simultaneously being something you can recreate for every audition, submission, or meeting you attend.

Style: Headshots are often informal and straightforward. They focus on the face, typically from the shoulders up or waist up, with minimal to no distractions in the background.

Composition: A headshot with a neutral or solid-colored background should be simple, emphasizing the artist's features. The artist's clothing should be clean and not distracting, with a focus on the face and eyes.

Preparation: Your photographer should know how to bring out your personality, but don't rely on them. When interviewing your photographer, inform them where your headshots will primarily be used and which roles resonate with you the most (e.g., musical theater, straight plays, TV/Film). Leading with this approach will help you and the makeup and hair artist (I highly recommend investing in a professional makeup and hair artist for your headshot session) to bring your personality forward with a polished look that will best accentuate you on camera.

Wardrobe: The wardrobe for headshots should be simple and free of distracting patterns or logos. Solid colors that complement your skin tone are best. The clothing should align with the type of roles you aspire to book.

The goal of your headshot is to establish a clear and professional image in the industry or to allow schools (colleges/universities) to reference you easily.

Lifestyle

If possible, find a photographer who understands both headshots and lifestyle shoots. The lifestyle part of a photo shoot will be another opportunity to highlight your special skills and personality. We discussed playing instruments in your performance reel section; please take some pictures of you with your instrument. Do you love visual art? Get a picture of you in action. These portraits can be used on your social media, website, and any self-produced project you make. Think of a lifestyle shoot as photographs of your special skills.

Both types of photos should be high-quality and taken by a professional photographer who understands the needs of professional performing artists. Poor-quality photos can undermine your image and sometimes prevent you from obtaining specific auditions.

Representation

Every performing artist asks about finding an agent or manager before they have secured and polished much of what we've discussed. So, if you've reached this point, you are ready for representation. Be mindful of the following when seeking representation.

Commission

Representation must be paid for their efforts in finding you jobs. Agents are generally paid 10% of your gross pay, while managers typically request 15%. Although these are standard minimum rates, some managers and agents have been known to negotiate for larger commissions. This compensation only comes when you book work. When working exclusively with an agent or manager, they will ask you to sign a contract. In my 21 years of experience, contracts usually last one to three (1-3) years. Managers sometimes offer five-year contracts if they want to work with you long-term.

If someone asks for money up front, RUN AWAY AND FAST!

Freelancing

This is when an agent or manager is interested in working with you but wants to "try out" the relationship before offering a contract. This does not require exclusivity with one agent or manager. I highly recommend freelancing with multiple agents or managers before signing a contract. Additionally, freelancing is an excellent way to network and build relationships, regardless of whether you are in a union or not. When your representation secures an audition for you, you can discuss the experience afterward to guide you both moving forward.

Think of freelancing as dating. Date around enough and you should be able to find "The One." Once you see "The One," know that the commitment doesn't have to mean forever. Like a marriage, this is a working relationship. Unlike a marriage, this relationship has a clear and written document detailing the endpoint; you can explore other options at any time during your relationship, as long as you are professionally doing so and not in breach of your contract.

Not all agents and managers do everything under one roof. The larger agencies and managers have multiple agents who specialize in niche areas of the arts for their clients. Sometimes, this will lead to an artist being represented by several people under a single agency. For example, your agent primarily submits you for theater, not VoiceOver. In that case, in writing, you should be sure you can seek representation in VoiceOver if your theater agent does not offer it.

You are a business. The artist/agent relationship is a business relationship. It should be navigated with formality and respect while optimizing the strengths of both your agent's ability to get you in the rooms where it happens and your ability to be present in your body in those rooms.

Auditions

Ya Made It! Let's freakin' show 'em what ya got! There are several types of auditions. What is most important to remember is that you are auditioning the creative team as much as they are auditioning you. Not every audition will be a perfect fit, and that's okay. You get to decide where your artistic stamp is put. Choose wisely.

Open Calls

An open call, sometimes called a "cattle call," is a casting process where performers of all experience levels are invited to audition without prior appointment or invitation. These auditions can feel overwhelming, as hundreds or even thousands of artists might line up for a chance to be seen, creating an atmosphere of intense competition and limited opportunities for individual attention. The term "cattle call" reflects the impersonal nature of the process, where artists might feel more like numbers than individuals. For many performers, attending an open call can feel like playing the lottery — hoping your number will be drawn for a callback despite the odds being stacked against you.

This can turn what should be a professional job interview into a daunting and emotionally taxing experience, where the chance of being seen, let alone booking the job, feels as random as luck. If you attend an open call, bring items that will calm your nervous system and boost your spirits during a long day of waiting to be seen. My favorite items include books, foam rollers, meditation podcasts, journals, and coloring books. These are my favorite items because I can do them while keeping my ears open for notifications in the holding room or during an open call.

Union Calls

An open union call is a casting opportunity where members of an actor's union, such as Actors' Equity Association (AEA), can audition for upcoming productions, including Broadway, national tours, and regional shows.

These audition calls often feel like a traditional in-person job interview with a dash of high-stakes lottery luck. You will be surrounded by a sea of equally talented union members, all vying for a limited number of roles. The atmosphere can be exhilarating and nerve-wracking as you prepare to give your all in a brief audition slot (usually 5-10 minutes in the audition room for singer/actors and 30-50 minutes for dance/movement calls), knowing that the competition is fierce. The odds can seem as random as a draw from a hat.

These auditions can sometimes include sides or materials; however, more commonly, if you're asked to stay around for additional rounds of auditions, you'll be provided with sides to bring back to a callback on another day.

In this scenario, success often hinges on a combination of preparation, timing, and luck, making the process both a test of skill and a calculated roll of the dice.

Agent/Invited Calls

An agent or invited audition call can make artists feel valued and recognized in their craft. Open calls have hundreds of hopefuls seeking a coveted "spot." In contrast, an invited audition means that a casting director, producer, or agent has requested to see you, and they will only call in a select number of people from the agents' offices and online casting websites they've pre-selected.

These auditions are often scheduled with specific appointment times, which allows for a more personalized and focused experience. Unlike open calls, where time is limited, an invited audition usually lets you showcase your abilities more fully. You can receive detailed feedback and take direction, allowing for adjustments to your performance based on notes from the room's creative team and casting directors. Additionally, the materials for the audition are usually sent to you in advance, allowing you time to prepare and present your best work thoroughly.

This setup isn't always ideal, but when it is, it allows for a more meaningful exchange during the audition.

As you work towards a career performing on Broadway stages and platforms that will illuminate your awesomeness, I hope you remember that auditions are steady progress made over extended periods. So, take your time and exhale through the journey.

4

Networking & Connections

An artist's preparation has everything to do with readying your-self for this part. There are many ways to network and make connections that don't feel like you're selling your soul. My favorite ways are:

- **Broadway Open Mic Nights:** I loved going to *Jim Caruso's Cast Party* when I began my career. I sang my face off there on many a Monday night. When I started working, I found solace in the splendor of community in places like Broadway Sessions w/Ben Cameron and open mic nights at The Duplex in the West Village. Open mic nights are a place to perform whether you're in a show or not. They're a place to meet new artists and co-create a space simply for the love of playing with your creativity.
- You guessed it, **CLASS**! When I take (and teach) classes at Steps on Broadway, Broadway Dance Center, or Peridance Center, I can count on meeting at least two (2) new artists every class. That doesn't sound like a lot, but it created a network of artists I grew alongside over time. Acting classes are where I made friends who were interested in creating their own works. Group Vocal Coaching is where I found friends who enhanced my musical tastes and where I found friends to attend shows and concerts with.

My love for producing began in acting classes. I still have

friends from my improv classes at <u>UCB</u> and <u>The PIT</u>, highlighting how developing an artistic community can ground and uplift you. If there is ever a group of people who understand what you're artistically going through, it is the people you'll meet in class. The *life* side of the relationships made there will enhance the work you perform and create while also affording you communal exhalation.

- **Auditions:** When you're in the holding room waiting to be seen, it's a perfect time to meet new people. Get to know your fellow artists and connect in the shared journey of auditioning.
- **Social Media:** YUP! Following artists who inspire you can lead to a connection in real life! I love meeting new people, especially when I follow them and meet the person only to see that we totally align and are like long lost artist friends! It makes me GEEKED!
- **Independent Theater Companies:** Joining collectives will bring artists together in a way that combines the best of what we individually do with the best things others do, to make a team of artists who are, dare I say, Fearless collectively.

When I moved to NYC at 19, I made a lifelong friend in Yusaf Nasir. This artist and I both worked as work-study at Steps on Broadway. There, he and I took so many classes we could barely walk home sometimes. On our shaky leg walks to the subway, he and I would talk about everything under the sun that happened on our shift, in our classes, the dreams we had, but mostly, we talked about why being a performing artist was so damn important to us.

As a young artist, I participated in dance competitions and conventions, where I met the best artists again! The most impactful relationship is that of my brother from another mother, Roderick George. He and I met at the NAACP ACT-SO competition. We immediately started loving each other's talents when we saw each other perform. For 23 years, he and I can go without talking for months, see each other, and pick up as if no time has been lost.

The best part about beginning your career is making these relationships. They will speak life into you in ways you can't initially imagine. That is what makes them so special: a bond of struggle and strength that will uplift you in and out of the audition room.

5

The Life of a Broadway Performer

B eing a Broadway artist is a dream for many, but it comes with as many unique challenges as it does rewards. Rigorous schedules, long hours, and a relentless pursuit of excellence characterize the life of a Broadway artist.

Artists must maintain peak physical and vocal condition to meet the demands of eight shows a week, often with only one day off. The preparation for each role involves countless hours of rehearsals, learning lines, perfecting choreography, and honing character development. Despite the physical and emotional toll, the thrill of stepping onto a Broadway stage, hearing the applause, and bringing stories to life in front of a live audience makes all of the work worthwhile. The camaraderie among cast members and the opportunity to continually grow as an artist are invaluable Broadway aspects.

However, the journey doesn't end when the curtain falls. Broadway performers must also navigate the complexities of life off-stage. Balancing the highs and lows in theater, managing relationships, and maintaining a personal life can be daunting.

The constant demand for excellence and the pressure to deliver night after night require a performer to develop resilience and adaptability. The life of a Broadway performer is a testament to passion, perseverance, and an unyielding commitment to your craft. It's a life where pursuing art is not just a job, it's a calling that can demand everything and sometimes not equally give back to you.

Staying Motivated & Resilient

The journey to and within Broadway is filled with outstanding triumphs but comes with its fair share of rejections and setbacks. Staying motivated and resilient through rejection is a common hurdle for artists.

First and foremost, remember that a "no" today doesn't mean a "no" forever.

When I began to understand that rejection is not a reflection of my talent, but rather a matter of someone's opinion of my compatibility for their show at that time. After my final audition for *The Lion King*. Which I auditioned for seven times over seven years.
It wasn't until my seventh audition and multiple callbacks later that I finally booked it. It was a dream come true and a reward I profoundly felt because I had held dear all the years of hard work and dedication that led to landing this show.

Because I didn't let the initial "no" deter me from seeking other places where I could find and feel the "Yes," it made for a softer landing when doors were not opening for me. It also made it all the sweeter when I finally did book the show.

Navigating Life in New York City

Living in New York City provides seemingly endless opportunities to immerse yourself in the arts, meet fellow creatives, and draw inspiration from everything surrounding you. However, the hustle and bustle of city life can also be overwhelming.

Finding suitable housing in NYC is the biggest hurdle. This hurdle requires careful planning and a willingness to compromise on space and location. Many NYC residents have roommates in neighborhoods further from the theater district to save on rent.

Keep in mind your proximity to reliable public transportation! Many NYC residents rely on the subways and buses, so I recommend allowing yourself a 30-minute buffer to arrive at your destination. Public transportation is not as reliable as your talent, and you don't want to make being late to rehearsals, classes, and shows a habit.

Fearless Friend, Plan Accordingly!

Financial considerations in the big city extend beyond just housing. The cost of living in New York City is among the highest in the United States, and budgeting is an essential skill. Broadway performers must manage their finances wisely and balance their incomes with the high cost of rent, food, transportation, and other living expenses like classes (drop-in or class cards - class cards are a way to buy dance or fitness classes in bulk. Many people find this to be a cost effective option), seeing shows, buying books, and/or continuing education, and most importantly, funds to LIVE YA LIFE! It is NYC, and you're young, gifted, and full of potential to make and create experiences that you'll add to the stories you'll tell.

Please factor in the unpredictability of income, especially when not engaged in a long-running show. Parents, this would be no different if your child were seeking a career in sales (real estate, medical supplies, etc.), which, funny enough, artists are salespeople.

Managing Finances

For artists, managing their finances is critical to building a sustainable career in the performing arts. Artists often take on side jobs or gigs to supplement their income, ensuring they can maintain their lifestyle and stay afloat between roles.

Budgeting is not just about managing day-to-day expenses but about planning for the future.

Creating a realistic budget that includes rent, utilities, transportation, food, and other necessities is essential while setting aside money for savings/emergencies, as well as fun. Understanding the financial realities of a Broadway career means recognizing that even when you book the job, the work is often temporary.

There will be gaps between gigs. Therefore, it's essential to avoid overspending during peak earning periods and to be prepared for the lean times.

Review the Unavoidable Costs Chart by following the link at the front of the book.

UNAVOIDABLE COSTS CHART

Investing in yourself, such as taking classes, attending workshops, and maintaining your physical and mental health, is a lifelong journey for an artist. These expenses are necessary for your artistic growth and should be factored into your budget.

Artists should move to The City with mindfulness and consideration of secure health insurance options. You are walking around NYC with your instrument; you must ensure you and your instrument can survive and thrive, so be prepared to care for it at all times. This includes maintaining insurance to care for yourself/instrument.

Taxes

Understanding taxes, particularly as a freelancer or independent contractor, is vital for performing artists. By managing finances wisely, artists can reduce stress, focus more on their craft, and build a creative and financially fulfilling career.

Maintaining Motivation Through Financial Ups and Downs

While artistic passion fuels your journey, the realities of financial instability can challenge even the strongest spirit. Broadway contracts, regional work, tours, and teaching gigs often fluctuate, making it vital to build a healthy relationship with money early on. It's important to remember that financial hardship is not a personal failure — it's part of the industry and your life, ebbing and flowing. Motivation during lean seasons is maintained by dreaming big and actively planning for sustainability.

Creating a monthly budget, saving during prosperous times, seeking side work that nurtures your creativity (like teaching or choreography), and viewing financial planning as part of your artistry are key to remaining resilient.

Money may not be why you started this journey, but respecting your financial well-being is a significant component of continuing your journey of being a fearless artist and independent adult.

A huge inspiration to me on finances comes from Ramit Sethi, whose work teaches me that motivation thrives when you remove the fear and shame surrounding money and replace it with intention, preparation, and self-compassion.

Staying ready offstage emotionally (with ease), artistically (with flow), and financially (with connectivity) ensures you're available to say "yes" when the opportunity calls.

Practicing balance in all aspects of life makes what we do seem easy, breezy, and cool! Your daily commitment to finding balance makes your fearless artistry's life take flight.

Balancing Work and Life

Managing a Broadway or Off-Broadway schedule demands a delicate balance between work and personal life. Artists must find ways to rest, recharge, and recover despite the demanding hours. Establishing a routine that includes proper nutrition, regular exercise, and sufficient sleep is crucial for maintaining physical and mental health.

Time management skills are essential to ensure that rehearsals, performances, and personal time are all given appropriate attention. Finding moments of relaxation and engaging in activities outside the theater can help maintain balance and prevent burnout. Audra McDonald may have all the Tonys, but she still has to find time to kick it and chill.

No matter the stage you're at, balance is the secret weapon to your success.

Mental and emotional health on a Broadway schedule can take its toll on a person in this high-pressure environment. The intensity of the work, coupled with the inevitable ups and downs of a career in the arts, can also take a toll on our well-being. Again, FYA Studios is a strong support network of fellow artists who are excited to welcome you into our community and help you understand how to navigate these challenges. Balancing work and life is about prioritizing your health and happiness while pursuing your passion.

To maintain a positive mindset, celebrate every small victory. If you do, the big milestones will be easy to applaud.

Take Breaks

The best thing I've done in my 21-year career journey is to temporarily walk away from the stage. This career is not a sprint; it's a marathon.

The first break I took was just after I married my wife. I wanted to live life, not on an 8-show-a-week schedule. I'm grateful we took that break and that I rested from the hustle of artist life. It helped me find a newfound passion for my craft. It also led me to continuing education, improving my relationships, and the opportunity to become an educator in the arts.

My second break came when I became pregnant. Although I continued producing shows and performing, I could not dance at as high a rate as before. Less physical movement taught me to lean into the beautiful and exhausting nature of creating a human in my body with as little additional physical stress as possible.

The third break was a forced one during the global pandemic, which shut down Broadway for over a year. During this time, I learned the value of family. Additionally, I began to set new goals and dreams. Many of these dreams and goals have come true, and many have been exceeded.

The answers I've found in the breaks and pauses of my career have given me the confidence and empowerment I needed to start a business, write, and share my writing, while learning to trust the inspirational sparks when they came.

I am Fearless today, but I can and will rest.

Breaks will enhance your resilience in this career. If you can honor yourself first, your journey will be richer than you imagine.

Not for nothing, the industry largely stayed the same when I left and came back. The Peter Allen song "Everything Old is New Again" is playing loudly in my ears as I write this. There will always be a new show coming into a Broadway house. There will always be an audition somewhere in New York City. So when you make the boss move to take a pause so you can come back better, more rested, and more insightful to what you need from your art and craft, you'll find that the business can and will align with where you are in the journey.

6

Parental Support & Self-Empowerment

Supporting your young artist's passion is a journey that demands both encouragement and understanding from you, the parent. Your role is crucial in nurturing their dreams and providing the emotional resilience needed as they navigate the inevitable highs and lows of a performing arts career. This support shows up in how you celebrate their successes, help them persevere through setbacks, and invest — financially and emotionally — in their future. As the parent of a young artist, you are the seed investor of a start-up company: your child's talent and future career.

By creating an environment where your child feels emotionally secure (ease), financially literate (flow), and mentally empowered (connectivity), you are giving them a well-rounded foundation for adulthood. At its core, a career in the performing arts is a life spent working in sales, but the product offered is your child's unique talent and artistry.

Think of it like this: when you hire a realtor to help you buy a home, their mission is to *ease* the house-hunting process, move with the market *flow*, and *connect* you with a space where you can live freely and fully. In the same way, an actor must cultivate ease in their body, flow with creative energy, and connect with the audience (or creative teams in auditions) through their craft. The actor is constantly "house-hunting" for themselves, seeking stages, roles, and opportunities where their artistry can root them into a theatrical home for a specified amount of time. And when they find the right theatrical "home," they don't just move in, they invite hundreds of people at a time to step inside and experience their unforgettable home furnishing — music, lights, sound, costumes, choreography, scenes, and transitions.

And just like a home, there will be times you walk in and don't like the decor or vibe of the space; the same is true for the theater. It's okay if someone doesn't like your show, as long as you do, you're set.

Be the Example

Parents play a vital role in shaping how their child perceives and responds to both victories and setbacks in the journey of being a performer. Celebrating small victories, such as mastering a challenging routine or landing a minor role, is crucial for building your child's confidence and resilience.

Parents can do this by getting involved! When your young artist learns a new dance or vocal technique, ask them questions that lead to dialogue.

Before you roll your eyes, as a parent, I know getting our kiddos to talk to us can be a Whole Thing. But the moments post-class and rehearsal are prime time for feedback. Leading questions can sound like:

- "Is there anything you've discovered about yourself while practicing or rehearsing XYZ?"
- "What part of today's class was the most interesting to you?"
- "Who or what inspires you to keep practicing and improving? Because I am noticing your growth in every rehearsal and class you take!"

Sometimes, I'll have parents sit in on private lessons, and I hear them say, "I say that all the time." Parents, I know you do! The goal is to get your young artist to hear you. Even if we say the same or similar things, we always come from the angle of leading dialogue and encouragement. Examples of this are:

- "That's a great point, and I feel that when I'm…"
- "Where does that resonate in your body? Because I am feeling that *(insert where you feel this within your body)*…"
- (To the teacher) "How long did it take you to learn….?"

When all else fails, if you're watching a private lesson or class, or rehearsal, and it's clear to you that your young artist is "over you," this is an excellent opportunity to drop a line like:

- "It looks like you're really getting this. I'm going to take a walk and reflect on all these gems." (Then return toward the end!)

Prompts like these can get your young artist talking and may even get them to ask about you, which brings me to my next point!

Share your journey

In my 12 years of teaching and coaching young artists, I've found that parents who learn new things alongside their children will expand the young artists' explorations in the studio.

I am not advocating for you to run a marathon or become a Michelin-star chef, but learning anything similar to their focus in the arts can bring newfound enthusiasm in class for both you and them! Examples of new skills parents have explored while I worked with their young artist include:

- Taking a dance class
- Musical game apps (particularly musical theory)

- Reading plays in a book club
- Meditation, foam rolling, and stretching
- Car karaoke games
- Taking cooking classes as a family
- Financial education as a family

These are just a few ideas, so allow your imagination and personal tastes to inspire you.

I'd be remiss if I didn't mention that all these classes are offered through Fearless Young Artists Studios in Harlem, NYC.

If they see you are inspired, they'll become inspired. They will open up more with their teachers and peers and within their work as artists. It will be crucial as they grow older and experience bigger milestones, accomplishments, and setbacks.

Shark Tank **Your Kids**

I love this show; it is the best tool for helping young artists understand the investment in their studies.

At slower times in the family schedule, sit them down and lay out a "pitch" for why you're investing in them and how and where they can begin to contribute to their business. This will help them to see how they can scale their art.

At slower times in *their* schedule, grab a snack, sit down together, and have *them* build a "pitch" for why you should continue investing. What are the returns they've experienced because of your initial investment of financial and emotional support, and how are they planning to invest in themselves?

Here, we are not only sharpening our minds as a business but additionally practicing gratitude, as many of the returns will be feelings, breakthroughs, and insights into learning before the "big payoff" or, as a student artist once said to me, "before I get drafted to Broadway."

This isn't about a big, scary dollar amount. It's about learning to think like a business owner because *you* are the business as a performing artist. You are teaching your young artist how to dream with a plan.

Even though the heart is where a dream starts, it also begins within our mindsets.

Here's a playful example, inspired by my journey:

Pitch Example

Hello Shark Mama,

My name is LaQuet Sharnell Pringle, and I'm here today seeking your belief and support as I build my Broadway career.

Your investment — whether it's a few hundred dollars for classes or a few (cough with confidence) hundred thousand dollars for college — will help fuel my training in dance, voice, and acting, and fund key career-building steps like:

- Attending live performances to study industry professionals in real time.
- Learning directly from top choreographers and directors through masterclasses.
- Investing in audition outfits that help me show up looking and feeling like a pro!
- Prioritizing my mental health so I can thrive creatively and personally.

I'm not just asking for support. I'm promising commitment.

I plan to find part-time work in theaters, gyms, dance/fitness studios, or small businesses within our community to contribute to my growth, build connections, and repay this investment before graduation through outstanding grades and continual and steady growth over the next four years of college and post-college.

The goal? I want to become a self-sustaining artist ready to book professional work, give back to my community, and continue my personal growth. I'm inviting you to invest not just in my talent but also in my dedication to building a career that will endure in any field that accentuates my creativity.

Thank you for believing in me — now let's make some magic happen.

Why this exercise matters

Building a pitch helps young artists understand that their dream isn't just emotional — it's a real, tangible project that takes time, care, and thoughtful planning. It shows them how to think like entrepreneurs. Because entrepreneurs are dreamers! And the best part? Your child will realize it's not just about money — it's about mindset, work ethic, and creating opportunities, which spotlights the business savvy one needs to shine every season.

Artists who are creative and strategic build long, fulfilling careers. It all starts with learning how to pitch their dreams to you, themselves, and the world.

And because every savvy business owner looks for ways to lighten their financial load, let's explore scholarships, grants, and other funding opportunities.

Scholarships, Grants, and Financial Assistance

When pursuing a career on Broadway, performing artists often face the challenge of funding their education, training, and career development. Various scholarships, grants, and financial aid programs are designed to support aspiring Broadway performers. Below is a list of opportunities and tips for applying to ensure you maximize your chances of receiving financial support.

1. The Princess Grace Foundation – USA

The Princess Grace Awards provide scholarships, apprenticeships, and fellowships to emerging theater, dance, and film performing artists. They support both students and early-career artists through training and performance opportunities.

- Eligibility: Students enrolled in professional training programs or early-career professionals.

2. The American Theatre Wing Scholarships

The American Theatre Wing, the organization behind the Tony Awards, offers scholarships to support young theater professionals. Their Jonathan Larson Grant, specifically, promotes musical theater composers, lyricists, and book writers.

- Eligibility: Young theater professionals and students.

3. SAG-AFTRA Foundation Scholarship

SAG-AFTRA provides scholarships for members or their dependents pursuing performing arts education. These scholarships can be helpful for actors and performers who are members of the union.

- Eligibility: SAG-AFTRA members or their dependents.

4. The New York Foundation for the Arts (NYFA)

NYFA offers grants to individual artists and creators, including performing artists, to help with professional development, education, and production. These grants are particularly valuable for young artists transitioning into their professional careers.

- Eligibility: Individual artists in the performing arts.

5. The National YoungArts Foundation

YoungArts provides financial awards, mentorship, and professional development to young artists between the ages of 15 and 18. Winners receive scholarships, and top performers are invited to participate in workshops with leading artists.

- Eligibility: Young performers between 15 and 18 years old.

6. College Scholarships for Performing Arts Majors

Many colleges with robust theater and performing arts programs offer scholarships to talented students. Notable programs include The Juilliard School, NYU Tisch, Carnegie Mellon University, and the University of Michigan. These programs offer merit-based and need-based scholarships.

- Eligibility: Prospective or current students in performing arts programs.
- Website: Check individual university financial aid pages.

7. The Entertainment Community Fund

The Entertainment Community Fund provides emergency financial assistance to performing artists facing economic hardships. While this is not a traditional scholarship, it offers a safety net for working artists in financial need.

- Eligibility: Professional performing artists.

8. Jacob's Pillow Scholarships

For aspiring dancers, Jacob's Pillow Dance Festival has offered scholarships to cover tuition for its renowned dance programs, which provide intensive training with some of the world's top choreographers. I was a scholarship recipient in 2002 and attended the Cultural Traditions: Katherine Dunham Legacy Intensive, which was one of the best experiences of my artistic career.

- Eligibility: Check Jacob's Pillow website for more information.

Resources for Funding Education and Training

- Dance/USA Fellowships to Artists (DFA) – Supports artists through financial awards and mentorship.

- Theatre Communications Group (TCG) – Fellowships and Funding– Provides fellowships for early-career actors, directors, and theater professionals.

Tips for Applying for Scholarships and Grants

1. **Start Early and Research Thoroughly**
Begin your search for scholarships and grants early to give yourself enough time to gather the necessary materials and submit well-prepared applications. Research multiple funding opportunities to find those that align best with your needs and artistic goals.

2. Tailor Each Application
Don't submit the same generic application to every scholarship or grant. Tailor your responses to match each funding body's values, mission, and requirements. Make sure to highlight why you are a good fit for their support.

3. Highlight Your Passion and Dedication
In your essays or statements, emphasize your commitment to the performing arts and future goals. Discuss how the scholarship will help you grow artistically and professionally, and show your passion for your craft.

4. Submit High-Quality Supporting Materials
Many scholarships require performance videos, headshots, or letters of recommendation. Ensure that your materials are professional and polished, and present the best version of your skills. Select videos that showcase your versatility and strengths. But you already know and have this if you've gotten this far in the book.

5. Stay Organized and Meet Deadlines

Keep a calendar or spreadsheet of all scholarship and grant deadlines. Missing a deadline can cost you a valuable opportunity, so submit your applications on time and confirm that all documents have been received.

6. Seek Feedback:

Before applying, ask a teacher, mentor, peer, or artistic coach to review your materials. A fresh pair of eyes can catch errors or offer suggestions to strengthen your application.

By exploring the various scholarships, grants, and funding opportunities and using these application tips, performing artists can secure the financial support they need to pursue their Broadway dreams.

Recommended Reading & Viewing

A successful artist reads — and they read a lot!

I didn't think I was a big reader when I was a kid. Then I realized that when I read something, I saw things in life that reminded me of what I'd read. This served as the epicenter of finding connectivity in my learning. Since that discovery, when I read today, I seek to learn when other artists experienced ease, flow, and connectivity in their journey. Given that you are reading this book, I know you strive to be in a community of artists who seek fearlessness in their professional and personal lives. These recommended books have helped me write this book, develop my voice as an artist, and find objectivity when approaching others' work.

Books to Inspire the Process

- "Letters to a Young Poet" by Rainer Maria Rilke
- "The Creative Habit" by Twyla Tharp
- "The Creative Act: A Way of Being" by Rick Rubin
- "The War of Art" by Steven Pressfield

- "The Artist's Way" by Julia Cameron

Books to Develop Performance

- "How To Tell A Story: The Essential Guide to Memorable Storytelling"
- "Grit: The Power of Passion and Perseverance" by Angela Duckworth
- "The Actor's Art and Craft" by William Esper and Damon DiMarco
- "The Unlimited Actor" by Nancy Mayans

Books to Empower Creativity

- "Big Magic: Creative Living Beyond Fear" by Elizabeth Gilbert
- "Think Again" by Adam Grant
- "Start With Why" by Simon Sinek
- "The Gifts of Imperfection" by Brené Brown

For many, the best community you have access to is your family. Some will find community and support through the company of books and scholarships, or your chosen family/community could be your support system.

All this can be found at Fearless Young Artists Studios. What you have read within these pages is a glimpse into the dialogues shared in our community.

7

THE BIG Step

Friend, the call you have dreamed of for years has finally come in, and you are making your Broadway Debut! WOO HOO! Here, we'll explore some final tips before stepping onto the stage, what to expect in rehearsals, the difference between being an original cast member versus a replacement cast member, maintaining longevity, and giving back.

So You're on Broadway, Now What? When you hang up the phone with your agent or the casting director, you should first sit and meditate! Now you can reflect on all the years of training, classes, books read, tears shed, financial uncertainty, and EXHALE through a new process of joy with your continued hard work and grounded-ness.

Original Cast

Okay, now you may call your friends and family. Stay on top of your emails as your first Broadway contract comes with a script, score, and sometimes musical tracks for vocal parts. I say sometimes because there have been Broadway shows I've done when a contract, script, score, or musical tracks have not come until weeks into the process. *(This is not customary, and the Actor's Equity Association works hard to prevent this from happening, but there are times when it does, so I've added this as a caveat to the rule.)*

So, let's assume you have everything before you begin.

As you open your script and score, read it entirely before high-lighting your lines. This will give you a good idea of the show and allow your imagination to play. You booked this show for a reason, and now you can explore its entire world, not just the audition sides. At the same time, remember the experience from the audition process. Bring with you to rehearsals *the paints* (your fearlessness) you utilized in your auditions, so you know how best to mix in on the canvas (the show).

Review any trouble spots you foresee when reviewing the score, then call your voice teacher. Acknowledging the hurdle before you begin rehearsals will allow you to be gracious with yourself when rehearsals begin.

Cast List

When you know the cast, start following them on social media! Get to know your "show family" before all the rehearsals begin, and you'll limit the social anxieties that can come when entering a new and life-changing experience.

If you're as big a nerd as I am (and because you're reading this, I assume you are), send someone a Direct Message on social media or an email and express how their work has connected with you. Perhaps you'll connect in real life, and if that happens, at this meetup, you could (and should) read the script together, chat about your audition experiences, or enjoy each other's company. This is especially helpful if you're a swing, understudy, or standby.

What are the roles?

Ensemble: An ensemble member in a Broadway show plays a crucial and dynamic role in bringing the production to life. Often referred to as "the backbone of the show," they support the principals by performing in large musical numbers, contributing to the musical and scenic atmosphere. The ensemble enhances the overall storytelling through dance, vocals, and acting. Ensemble members can play multiple roles, transitioning seamlessly between characters in various scenes while maintaining the energy and precision that elevate the entire production.

Beyond the onstage presence, ensemble members must master intricate choreography, hold down tight harmonies, and adapt to constant changes in staging and direction.

Ensemble members are often an understudy for principal roles, meaning they must be prepared to step in at a moment's notice.

Swings: A swing in a Broadway show is usually the most versatile and essential performing artist. They are responsible for covering (knowing) the entire ensemble's dialogue, singing parts, and choreography.

This is a bold but accurate statement because the swing has to know every dance specialty (lifts, lines, blocking, backstage transitions) and have costumes for every ensemble track (role). I have known swings that have covered up to six or seven people sporadically! This is not an easy job. When finding your flow in a role of this magnitude, please remember that TIME is what you need to manage and compartmentalize, knowing multiple tracks at once and being able to step into those roles at any given moment.

When an ensemble member calls out sick, takes a vacation, or is injured, swings step in and up — often with little notice and sometimes for multiple ensemble tracks in one performance.
A swing does not perform nightly, but must remain sharp and ready to jump in. Being a swing is undoubtedly one of the most demanding jobs in the theater.

Understudy: In a Broadway show, an understudy is a cast member who steps into a principal or featured (lead or supporting) role when the nightly performing actor is unable to perform.

An understudy must thoroughly learn the script, blocking, choreography, and nuances of the role they cover, often in tandem with their ensemble or swing responsibilities.

Being an understudy requires discipline and mental agility. As with swings, understudies can go on with little notice, sometimes learning of their performance just hours before a show. Despite the pressure, an understudy embodies the character with the same professionalism and artistry as the nightly performing artist. Being an ensemble or swing member can best sharpen your skills to be adaptable and playful.

Standby: A standby is an off-stage performer who specifically covers one (sometimes more) principal role(s). They do not appear in the show unless called upon, but must be ready at a moment's notice, often mastering a deep understanding of the script, score, blocking, and emotional life of the character.

Featured Ensemble: These performers are ensemble members highlighted at key moments — through solos, small scene work, or complex choreography — offering them moments to stand out while supporting the larger story of the show.

Featured Principals: (or Supporting Actors) These artists play characters who significantly impact the narrative, often appearing in multiple scenes and musical numbers, offering dimension and depth to the production.

Principal Roles: These artists carry the heart of the story. They lead the show through their characters' journey, anchoring the emotional, thematic, and narrative arcs with skill, presence, and stamina.

Whether offstage preparing or center stage leading the way, each role is crucial and interconnected and must be highly respected within a show's professional ecosystem to further its success.

Rehearsals

The rehearsal process is an eight- to nine-hour day with a one- or two-hour lunch break. Much of the day is spent in a large dance studio with phenomenal acoustics, sprung dance floors, a three-piece band (piano, drum set, and percussion), and a revolving door of various members of the creative team (director, choreographers, writers, musical directors, designers, producers) and close friends of the show.

On a typical day, the ensemble will learn one or two major musical numbers in the large dance studio while the leads (principals) will rehearse the book scenes in a smaller dance or rehearsal studio. Sometimes, the leads will jump back and forth between the studios to be added to musical numbers, so the agility of learning songs and scenes is critical when cast as a lead.

The rehearsal process is where the writing teams change and enhance their script and score. This means changes happen daily. It is common to go to lunch with one set of lines only to return with new pages of lines. Learning quickly is a top priority for Broadway performers, and this skill is put to the test during rehearsals and in the preview stages of putting up a Broadway show.

Previews

Previews serve as a bridge between rehearsals and the official Opening Night. After the technical elements (costumes, lights, sound, set, and any automation) have been added, it's time to perform in front of a live audience.

During this period, the creative team uses audience reactions and feedback to fine-tune the production. This includes adjusting pacing, altering dialogue, changing choreography, cutting, or adding entire scenes or musical numbers. It's a dynamic time when the cast, backstage crew, creative team, and producers work diligently to polish the show for Opening Night.

For the cast, the preview process can be both exciting and challenging. Performers make changes quickly, often rehearsing new material during the day and performing the new material in the show at night. This crucial time shapes the final product and ensures that by the time the show officially opens, the entire production team, cast, and crew can enjoy the Opening Night's beautiful and emotional roller coaster.

OPENING NIGHT!

The Opening Night of a new Broadway show is magical! It's a high-stakes event that evokes excitement, anticipation, and sometimes nerves, all in the culmination of years of hard work. It is a much-needed payoff for the cast, crew, and creative team who can finally present the production to an audience filled with celebrities, industry leaders, professionals, politicians, critics, and other theater enthusiasts.

The day of Opening Night, you will have to balance your personal excitement with the focus you'll need to actually perform. Before the curtain rises, you'll come to the theater as usual, but this day you'll probably arrive an hour or so earlier to prepare before the show. A half-hour before the half-hour call, there is a celebration onstage!

The celebration includes the Legacy Robe winner (an honor bestowed upon the ensemble member with the most Broadway credits), an acknowledgment of the Broadway debuts in the cast, and speeches from the producers and creative team. After all this has happened, it is time for the half-hour call to the official Opening Night!

The energy backstage is electric, with performers making last-minute preparations, getting into costume, looking through your Opening Night gifts, and my personal favorite: eating the yummy treats brought in to celebrate the night. All while the audience fills their seats, buzzing with anticipation. No matter the result, a shared infectious and fearlessly radiant energy surges through every person in the theater. When the curtain rises, the cast exhales like an Olympian walking into the arena ready to compete. At the same time, the audience inhales with the hope and excitement of being carried into a world of fabulous imagination.

Opening Night is also when the reviews will be published. Sometimes, they come in as the show is happening. Whatever the reviews say, YOU DID THAT! This show is happening, and at every turn, you should pat yourself on the back for the herculean feat it is to open a Broadway show. Also, instead of worrying about the reviews, think about how fantastic you'll look in your Opening Night outfit at the after-party instead! Here, you'll have the famous step and repeat photo line, a lavish party, the opportunity to mingle with celebrities, producers, and invited fans, toasting the success of the night and the journey ahead.

There is one more element of booking your first Broadway or major role, and that is being a replacement. This often does not come with the experience of a full studio rehearsal for eight to nine hours, a technical rehearsal, or an Opening Night with all the majesty described above.

Replacements: Replacing another actor during a Broadway run can be exhilarating and challenging for an artist. Stepping into an established role means the actor must quickly adapt to the rhythms and dynamics of a show that's already running.

The rehearsal process is shortened to four to five hours during the day before the evening show. The dance captain, stage management, or, in some exceptional cases, a resident director or choreographer, leads these rehearsals. An actor who is a replacement should prepare to have solo or private music rehearsals with the musical director, attend costume and shoe fittings, and then return to rehearsals before heading to the theater in the evening to watch the show.

The more fun moments of being a replacement come with lobby rehearsals. A lobby rehearsal happens when the show is in progress onstage and the dance captains, swings, and any off-stage covers review and practice the choreography at the show's tempo in the theater lobby. This lobby time always happens during the show.

In between numbers, the dance captain reviews notes and blocking. This ensures that you are show-ready when you go into the show. Lobby rehearsals usually happen after several in-studio rehearsals or in tandem with your studio rehearsal. Rehearsing the show in the lobby allows you to find and understand the show's flow and continuity in real time. Often, the swings will join you in these lobby rehearsals, allowing your first time running through the show to be done with more people around you.

Finally, while no Opening Night celebrations come with being a replacement, that should not stop you from being excited about going into the show.

To begin, there will be a "Put In" rehearsal onstage. HOPEFULLY!

This is where you'll have all your costumes, technical elements, and full cast to give you as close to the show experience as possible before your first experience with a paying audience. Generally, the Put In happens a day (or so) before you perform officially. In some cases, it's the same day. Your job is to roll with the punches and remember to make contact with your breath by inhaling and exhaling with ease, flow, and connectivity.

In a few short weeks, you would have become familiar with the script, blocking, choreography, and the emotional nuances and relationships already built onstage. You can step into a character created by someone else and make it your own. The best replacement cast members find places to redefine their newfound tracks. It's a test of an actor's resilience and craft. One that can be deeply rewarding both personally and professionally.

Maintaining Longevity in Your Career

A Broadway performer's recovery team is essential to sustaining the rigorous demands of performing eight weekly shows. Given the high intensity of Broadway shows, maintaining physical and mental well-being involves a robust support system to ensure one can stay in peak nightly performance condition.

This team typically includes a physical therapist, massage therapist, vocal teacher, vocal coach, and sometimes a chiropractor and acupuncturist to help manage the physical strain, prevent injuries, and address any issues that arise from repetitive movements. These specialists work to enable both the performer's longevity in the show and career.

In addition to physical care, a Broadway performer's recovery team may include mental health professionals, such as a therapist or performance coach. The emotional and psychological toll of performing at such a high level, coupled with the pressures of the industry, can lead to burnout or mental exhaustion.

Regular therapy, or mindfulness coaching, helps performers manage stress, build resilience, and maintain a healthy mindset, allowing you to bring your best self to the stage without feeling overwhelmed.

Nutritional guidance also plays a crucial role, as many performers work with dietitians or nutritionists to fuel their bodies healthily.

Rest and recovery are massively important. Injuries happen most when you're tired. Artists can take yoga, meditation, or sleep therapy classes for active recovery and rest. This holistic approach helps artists balance the intensities of performing six days a week with eight shows during that week.

A well-rounded recovery team is vital for managing the physical demands of the job and maintaining mental clarity, emotional well-being, and long-term success in the performing arts.

I should mention that all of this is financially covered through the artists' weekly pay. Hence, why I suggested you understand the financial demands of being an artist in training in the earlier sections. This will only enhance the experience of achieving and living out your dreams.

Giving Back

By integrating philanthropy into your performing schedules, you can enrich your life, knowing that your work entertains audiences and makes a tangible difference.

For a Broadway performer, finding a meaningful cause to support while working on a show can provide a sense of purpose beyond the stage. Performing in a Broadway production is physically and emotionally demanding, but aligning with a cause, whether related to the arts, education, mental health, or social justice, can offer a way for a performer to connect their craft with a larger mission.

Many Broadway artists get involved with organizations like Broadway Cares/Equity Fights AIDS, R.Evolucion Latina, Broadway Serves, Broadway Baby Mommas & Broadway Babysitters, The Lesbian, Gay, Bisexual & Transgender Community Center to name a few, Philanthropy allows artists to use their platform to raise awareness and funds for critical issues the have significant meaning to the artist.

When not performing in a Broadway show, a cause provides structure, motivation, and fulfillment during gaps in work. Many performers use their downtime to volunteer, organize charity events, or advocate for important causes. This balance between artistic expression and social impact helps performing artists stay grounded, resilient, and connected to the world around them.

8

Putting It All Together

At some point, a teacher, parent, or someone in your community has said, "You should write your own show!" Perhaps you've heard "Create your own work to get your foot in the door." All of this is fair and true. However, when you're entering college, getting ready to graduate, or have just begun your journey auditioning, knowing where to start when creating your work can seem daunting. To be clear, creating your work is 'A Whole Thing,' but something that can help you discover, define, and differentiate yourself from other artists. It can also lead you towards performing opportunities that are unique to your talents and passions.

This chapter aims to lower the pressure associated with beginning to create your work. It doesn't mean you need to jump right into writing the next big Broadway musical, but it can lower the stakes of approaching what you can create while pursuing other performing opportunities.

I'll walk you through the initial steps of bringing your original ideas to life. Whether you're a dancer with a vision, a poet with a play inside you, or a composer ready to shape a score, this section will provide practical tools.

Don't wait or ask for permission to make art. The industry's future belongs to those bold enough to build stages for themselves.

Why self-producing is essential for a modern performer

It is impossible to be an artist and not create. If you are audacious enough to call yourself an artist, you better add "fearless" in front of "artist." Whether you're creating for social media (YouTube, Instagram, TikTok, etc), teaching, composing, or writing, it's all a form of creating something that needs to be shared with your community. Could you begin creating without a plan in place? Yup! But without a plan, you'll surely burn out or become so stressed by the process that you give up.

When artists are awake and aware of their creative process, they are more likely to keep creating. The skill of self-production will attract more eyes to your work and bring you closer to achieving your artistic goals and dreams.

It's common for casting directors, choreographers, directors, and others to check out an artist on their social media or website before bringing them in for an audition. So, the work you create and share often leads to career opportunities.

In fact, I've secured dozens of jobs from the strength of what I've created on my social media and website. This is helpful because I don't have to tell people who I am. I can come into a

space with folks who already understand who I am, what inspires me, my creative process, my point of view, and, most importantly, WHY I create.

Aligning your identity with your art - Culture, Activism, & Joy

One of the most misconceived notions about being a performer is that we have to wait until we're "famous" to use our platforms to speak up and out about the issues that matter to us.

NOT TODAY, FEARLESS FRIENDS!

What you care about is directly connected to the work you can create. The million-dollar question is, What lights you up? As long as you can approach what aligns with you in a way that pulls people into what you care about, you are ready to start self-producing.

Artists who have done this include Marti Gould Cummings (actor and political activist), Katie Webber (lifestyle, plant-forward eating, and recipes), and Marla Louissaint (culture is at the center of all things performing and political).

Find Your inspiration to develop an original work

Your inspiration to create resides in your Why. I love creating. Painting, writing, choreography, and scene work represent my passion for problem-solving. I love to create because I love finding fun ways to solve problems. Home renovation shows are one of my favorite things to watch because the shows are about seeking creative solutions to unforeseen problems.

My work is inspired by solving something or, at the very least, introducing a conversation that will lead toward the problem being solved.

Finding your inspiration is attainable by practicing the High Five Approach.

I.R.V.L.T - Imagination, Risk, Voice, Legacy, Truth

1. **Your Imagination**: Here are some questions that will help you identify recurring creative themes that may become the seeds for your next project: *What story, idea, or emotion calls or continually pulls you into daydreaming?*
2. **Taking Risks** can ground your work in empathy and connection while aligning with your desire for impact. - *If you could create a piece that would make one person in your community feel seen, healed, or heard, what would it be about?*
3. **Your Voice** can help tap into your personal truth (point of view) as a source of creative authenticity. - *What's a moment*

from your life that you wish someone had captured in a scene, song, or monologue? What made it so powerful or transformational?

4. **Your Legacy** connects your art to the current world and opens the door to bold, timely work. - *What cultural, political, or social shifts do you feel deeply connected to — and how might you artistically respond to them?*

5. **Your Truth** permits innovation, disruption, and dreaming beyond current and present societal norms. - *If you could make one kind of show, performance, or piece that doesn't currently exist — but should — what would it look, sound, or feel like?*

Many artists have the inspiration to tell a story, but they don't know how to bring it to life. Below are easy ways to follow through and begin to share your ideas.

1. Name the Spark Before You Explain It

Instead of diving into the full idea right away, start by naming what moved you:

- "What if a show opened with..."
- "There's this image I can't shake..."
- " I keep thinking about a story where..."

Naming the inspiration first relieves the pressure to have a fully formed concept. Once you name it, invite a friend into your creative energy, not your finished product. The goal is to share the emotion of the vision, not the $10 million production.

2. Share Your Spark as Curiosity, Not a Pitch
Try saying:

- "I'm not asking for feedback yet — I just want to say this out loud to hear how it feels. Once I'm done, will you 'Yes And' what you've heard by piggybacking off my initial spark idea?"

This sets boundaries and allows you to explore and not perform your idea. Your friend becomes a mirror, not a judge. This shift in mindset invites vulnerability and momentum.

3. Create a Ritual of Exchange

Choose one trusted friend and set a regular, low-stakes time where you both can bring an unfinished idea, lyric, sketch, or scene to share. Perhaps you can come up with a playful name like:

- "Idea Café"
- "Creative Sparks Exchange"
- "5-Minute Sparks"

When mutuality and consistency are part of the process, trust is built, and creative courage will develop over time.

Once you and a friend have bounced your ideas off of each other, you will begin to find Flow within the inspiration. This means that the idea is coming to life. This is a perfect time to expand upon the boundaries you've created by asking this friend (or another friend who crosses their T's in a slightly more formal way than your first friend) to help you plan a showing of the idea(s). Repeat these steps until the first scene, lyrics, dance, and painting come together. Then, begin sharing with more trusted friends.

9

Building a Business as an Artist

Y ou Are the Brand and the Business. You are the one going to the auditions, making the connections, creating new works, sharpening your tools, and that is NO DIFFERENT than any other entrepreneurship.

When I began calling myself a creative entrepreneur, I felt more confident about navigating the roads ahead because my mindset shifted to what drives me to wake in the morning: creating. I want to find as many ways to design and develop a new and exciting repertoire for my performing company, which will add to the cultural fabric of my community. It's not enough that I got some fabulous professional opportunities if I'm not passing the baton to the next generation. Doing this while running my race is the long game of successful and innovative entrepreneurs.

My business has evolved over 20+ years, so when people ask if there is a sustainable life within the arts, ask them how many companies do they know that have been open as long as I've been working in the performing arts? Longevity in *any* career is commendable and a testament to learning how to find and apply Ease, Flow, and Connectivity in your professional and personal life. Why do you think those "super-rich people" are always seemingly on vacation? Like it or not, they are practicing finding Ease and Flow in Connection to themselves.

They, and you, are building the tools to lead your personal and professional relationships with continued success of learning how to Optimize, Navigate, Strengthen, Evolve, and Transform, also known as scaling your business over an extended amount of time. But here at FYA Studios, we refer to this as The Onset Technique.

So, let's get started artistically applying the model of a startup company to the first decade of your professional life. That is to say, each of the following sections will speak to understanding yourself as a personal brand.

Business formation brings your dreams to reality

- Building your audience through storytelling and service
- Taxes, write-offs, and financial systems
- Contracts, LLCs, and when to hire professionals
- Passive income for artists (coaching, digital courses, teaching, merchandise)

Whether you've just graduated from high school or had your first Broadway credit, these topics will empower you as a Creative Entrepreneur whose job it is to sell a particular set of skills (also known as your talent) to help solve a problem - bringing the story in someone else's mind to a stage in an articulate way.

Artist as Start-Up: Building Your Creative Business with Heart, Strategy, and Vision

Understanding Yourself as a Personal Brand

Before anyone buys a ticket to your show, follows your work, or hires you for a project, they must understand who you are and what you stand for. Your brand is not a logo, a tagline, or a perfectly curated Instagram feed. It's the feeling people get when they interact with you. It's your point of view, your values, your style, your presence — and yes, your skill set.

For dancers, your brand may be how you blend classical training with street or contemporary styles. For singers, it could be the texture of your voice paired with the type of stories you gravitate toward. For actors, your brand lives in your chosen roles, the scripts you write, and the causes you speak about. And for musical theater performers, it's the alchemy of your vocal tone, movement style, comedic timing, and with the kind of depth of heart that can soothe a Broadway theater audience's mind to completely engage (away from technology) to your fully engaged performance.

Start small: Ask yourself what themes you consistently bring into a room. What do directors, coaches, or friends always say about you? Who or what do you want your name to be synonymous with? Then, write a one-line brand promise:

"I am a _____ who brings _____ to every story I help to tell."

My one-line brand promise is: I am a **Creative Entrepreneur** who brings **visibility with ease, flow, and connectivity** to every story I help to tell.

You move with purpose when you know and can confidently express your identity. And when you move with purpose, people remember you.

Building Your Audience Through Storytelling & Service

Your audience doesn't need you to be famous — they need you to be real. One of the most potent ways to build a connection is through storytelling. As artists, you already do this on stage. Now it's time to do it offstage — on social media, in newsletters, in conversations, and in every space that you enter.

Don't post to impress. Post To Connect!

Tell a story about the audition that didn't go your way but taught you something. Share the behind-the-scenes process of your self-tape or rehearsal. Talk about your *why*. As you build this bridge of authenticity, people will be drawn to your journey and root for your success.

And when you show up in service, not just to get but to give, your community grows. Ask yourself: "How can I be helpful to myself and others today?" Whether recommending your favorite vocal warm-up or sharing a rehearsal tip, this generosity builds trust. That's how audiences form, not from vanity metrics but from meaningful moments.

Taxes, Write-Offs & Financial Systems

Your art is your business, and businesses need structure. Many artists avoid the topic of money because it feels scary or complex, but it's just another system to learn. Begin with a straightforward goal: track your income and expenses. A spreadsheet or app (like Quick-Books Self-Employed) is enough to start. *I am a massive fan of Intuit QuickBooks, and I am not paid to say that. And I pair this service with the insight, guidance, and professionalism of an artist who has 20 years of experience in accounting.*

Learn what counts as a write-off. When you work professionally, many artists and start-up businesses can deduct expenses that directly support your career. This includes:

- Acting/dance/singing classes
- Headshots and reels
- Union dues
- Audition travel
- Equipment (laptop, lighting, camera)
- Home office/studio space

- Coaching, therapy, or bodywork that supports performance

Save your receipts, label your categories, and keep a folder for each tax year! You don't need to become a CPA, but it is in your best interest to know the numbers behind your investment in launching your product (talent and gift) into the world.

Financial literacy is self-advocacy. Don't wait until you book a national tour to get your system in place. Start now, and your future self will thank you.

Again, KNOW YOUR NUMBERS!

Contracts, LLCs & When to Hire Professionals

As your career grows, your legal and business needs will evolve. Here's the key: don't wait until there's a problem to start protecting yourself. Every gig, no matter how small, deserves a written contract. It doesn't need to be pages long — it merely needs to outline expectations, compensation, deliverables, and timelines.

You may want to set up a business structure that benefits your numbers and is something you've discussed with a professional about your many options. Doing so can protect your assets, offer tax advantages, and help you be more professionally presented when applying for grants, residencies, or funding. A sound business structure is a smart next step to self-produce or build a brand that sells anything, like classes, merchandise, or any creative and artistic service you may offer.

This step in the process is one that I am most proud to help navigate with my coaching clients. I never claim to know it all, but I can make it a point to find those most qualified to do a job to help me do my job with Ease, Flow, and Connectivity.

When should you hire a professional?

- When the contract is complicated or high-stakes

- When setting up your business structure
- When you're unsure how to file your taxes correctly
- When negotiating pay, licensing, or usage rights

A 30-minute consult with a lawyer or accountant can save you thousands of dollars and a lot of stress. Companies and organizations such as Fractured Atlas or New Foundation for the Arts can help guide you to protect your work as an artistic human or, better yet, a Creative Entrepreneur who brings stories to life.

It won't be fun to lose your work after dedicating so much time and effort. SO PROTECT IT!

Passive Income for Artists:

Coaching, Courses, Teaching & Merchandise

Let's be real. No one wants to hustle every month to survive. You can build a creative career that supports your dreams *and* your life by exploring passive or supplemental income streams while creating something artistically simultaneously.

Here are ways you can earn that allow for some financial flexibility.

Popular Passive Streams of Income for the modern-day performing artists:

- Coaching or giving private lessons: voice, audition prep, dance, storytelling
- Creating digital courses or PDF guides: "My 5-Day Breath & Voice Warm-Up" or "How to Prep for a Summer Intensive"
- Merchandise: creating custom journals, affirmation cards, t-shirts
- Licensing your choreography or original music

- Writing E-books or filming video libraries of something you are highly skilled at doing and can teach.

The key is to create from your current strengths and repurpose what you already know. You don't need to be an influencer when you're too busy solving problems for your people, community, and network.

Building a creative business means showing up bold, brave, playful, and fearing a little less because you have a plan.

Build with intention. Experiment. OFTEN! Rest! Remember: You are the startup and the success story that will attract more business.

Check out the Workbook to help you get started.
Artist As a Startup & RampUp

10

Your Legacy

The performing arts are often described as a marathon, not a sprint. They don't tell you that the path isn't always straight and certainly isn't flat! It curves, climbs, dips, and doubles back on itself. Longevity in this career is less about enduring through exhaustion and more about building a relationship with your artistry that can evolve. It requires perspective, flexibility, and deep self-awareness. To sustain joy and a thriving career, you must learn to shape your path with intention, not just chase gigs until the tank is empty.

So, I invite you to plan your artistic life in chapters, not timelines. This approach allows you to acknowledge seasons of growth, stillness, reinvention, and transformation.

What does a five-year chapter look like for you? It could be focused on auditioning, building credits, and saying yes to every opportunity. The following 10-year chapter might include branching out into regional theater, international work, or starting to choreograph and assist.

Your 20-year chapter might look entirely different — directing, producing, creating original work, or even running a studio or company of your own.

When you map your career this way, you make space for your evolution without shame or urgency. It also allows you time to change your plans, which often happens as we evolve. Every chapter has a purpose in the overall telling of your story. In actor terms, this is a classic "Because of that, this happened. And then, because of that, the next thing happened." Looking at the story of your life as a creative human is to "Yes, And" yourself.

But nothing can flourish without rest.

Burnout is real, especially in an industry where you're often taught to push through, keep hustling, and never say no. Rest is not the opposite of ambition — it's the companion.

And because of that, the more intimate and connected you are to the companion that is rest, the more likely you are to give yourself the patience needed to dance through life.

Breaks allow for integration. They give you time to reflect, refuel, and reconnect with your *why*. Reinvention becomes possible when you step out of cruise control and make way for the peace of stillness that comes from taking in the scenery around you on the winding road you are driving on.

Some of the most powerful shifts in my career came after I permitted myself to pause. Fearing the quiet seasons is ultimately a fear of meeting your whole self. Use the quiet times to explore the parts of yourself that you don't make time for when you're booked or busy. Savor the quiet time. They are not a threat to your momentum but a foundation for your next chapter.

And maybe your next chapter isn't on stage. That doesn't mean you're any less of an artist. Some of the wealthiest, most fulfilling moments in this field happen when you step into another role — educator, director, choreographer, coach, writer, advocate, or mentor. If you've ever led a warm-up, staged a piece, offered a friend notes, or taught at a summer camp, you already have the instincts and are building the language for your next chapter.

The industry needs artists who can do more than perform.
It needs leaders.
Creators.

Visionaries.

You don't have to choose just one title for your entire life. The beauty of this field is that your artistry can wear many hats.

With time and experience comes a responsibility — and an opportunity — to give back. Mentorship, coaching, or simply showing up as a resource for the next generation has a profound impact on the community. It's how the industry gets better. It's how equity grows. It's how you anchor your growth in the community. Whether you're sharing knowledge in a masterclass, encouraging a younger artist backstage, or writing a guide like this, you're contributing to a legacy that ripples far beyond your journey.

It's not just about what you book, it's about what you build.

Legacy isn't about how famous you become. It's about how many people were better because you created. And it starts now. You affirm your art by honoring it every season, not just when the jobs roll in. There will be years when your life shifts — marriage, children, loss, health changes, creative droughts. In those seasons, you may not move, sing, or write as you used to. But your artistry still lives in you. It may shift forms. It may speak in whispers instead of roars, but it never disappears.

This chapter is about how you define your creative stamp when someone writes about you in the history books.

Imagine if Shakespeare had an iPhone. Fearless Friends, the content (The Works of Art)... I! MEAN! So, how do you stay connected to your craft through all the changing of seasons? You return to your ease, flow, and connectivity.

The root of The Onset Technique is the foundation of a fearless artist's life. Instead of performing from tension and survival, you learn to drop in.

You listen.

You build rituals of care into your work.

You move from your center, not your panic.

The goal is not to fight your body or the industry, it's to stay awake and aware of who you are.

This is your invitation to zoom out. To see your career as a living, breathing story, you get to co-write every day.

Check out the worksheet for help.

Legacy and Longevity Worksheet

Legacy Map, Reflections, and Annual Intentions

11

You're Fearless. I Can Hear Your Roar.

You're reading this because you have been gifted with an instrument. You must find the flow of your instrument because it will evolve. What you do at 16, 17, 18 will not necessarily be what you do in your 20s, 30s, 40s, and so on. At 16, I could sing a high B6 first thing in the morning. After singing on Broadway for close to a decade, my voice changed. I had a vocal injury that required surgery and recovery, and my voice now lives in a sensible mix belt of a G5...depending upon whether I want to sing that day.

What was true in the past may not be true for us now, and dwelling on what worked for us at 18 may delay our arrival at the physical, mental, emotional, and spiritual levels we need to be. I hope this book feels like a place that you courageously return to to witness and build your strength. But remember, artists must take risks. When pursuing a career in the performing arts, you must be fearless. That means being an artist who is ambitious and determined. I've shared practical and tactile tools I've gathered and utilized over 12 years of teaching, coaching, and mentoring artists thriving in various areas of the arts.

I offer and share this with you because I hope that every person who says they want to be an artist has all the tools and information needed to pursue and apply themselves towards having a creative life.

When you question yourself, positively or negatively, remember you are not alone. By acknowledging the doubt that steps in, you can create a new way of approaching the process of accomplishing your dreams.

From that place of acknowledgment, you then head towards reflection. When done correctly, reflection leads to ease within your instrument.

Things can and should change over time. Especially if what you're doing is being done in a way that is healthy and connected to the evolution of your instrument and artistry.

Our lives as artists and humans are about bravely aiming to connect what we've learned in the past (which includes what we learn daily) to our present selves. It is not our job to carry all of our past, present, and future at once, so drop what does not serve you any longer as you go. Embrace the now and glance at what's ahead.

If we were meant to stay the same artist forever, we wouldn't be very good at what we do.

To be a Fearless Young Artist for the rest of your life means acknowledging that your instrument's ease, flow, and connectivity will change over time.

Let's not forget that my desire to have more time led to writing this book. Patience is the single thing you can not buy, borrow, or loan. It is something you gift yourself and others. I choose to be an artist who lives freely and fearlessly. In every moment of the 12 years since I asked myself what my art could do for me, I have seen miracles happen daily.

From the young artists I've taught who grew up to find themselves in a position to hire *me* for work. Or artists who chose to collaborate their business with mine to benefit both of us. To the artists who are close friends on social media, which in our community means consistent shares and reposts, sending one another memes, LIKING

EVERYTHING, and virtual hugs on the days neither of us wanted to lift our heads from the pillow.

To my fellow fearless artists, who I've watched evolve and embrace the multi-hypenates they are, and creating and leaving a stamp of creative individuality within the world, Thank You for allowing me to see your growth. Your inspiration leaves a stamp of your artistic richness on my heart.

It's terrific to know artists who are parents, authors, community organizers, entrepreneurs, coaches, or—my favorite—committed to energetically and fearlessly showing up healed and present for everyone in their community, but always giving to themselves first!

The Arts are the best medicine we can take to heal ourselves, especially if we practice them with self-awareness, humility, and the ability to remain learners of life.

If we can show up to every aspect of our creatively lived life knowing how best to manage, regulate, and connect our instrument with others who choose to do the same, then we are well on our way to being bold, brave, playful, and fearless.

The world needs your voice and stories to shatter barriers and share joy with all humankind.

Be fearless by focusing on your goals and sharpening your tools with love and passion. Create from a place of truth and vulnerability — even when the ghost lights go down.

Because joy is meant for everyone.
My fearless friend,
Be Bold.
Be Brave.
Be Playful.

And Be Fearless, Together.

Bonus
So You've Read,
Becoming A Fearless Young Artist....

Watch how to apply it all.

As a 20-year performing arts veteran, building a practice to prepare my body for creative work has been central to my success and journey. As I've collected practices and techniques over my career, I've found myself creating The Onset Technique, a powerful approach to prepare your instrument vocally, physically, and emotionally for our work as actors in theater.

The best way to introduce you to this methodology is to do the work. Click, or check out the video below by following the website link below. To find resonance physically, vocally, and experiential.

VIDEO

Now that you've explored this introduction, repeat this video every day for 14 days. Your body will be ready to level up at the end of the two weeks. This can be done by joining our online FYA Studios community, where you can find incremental programs to follow along with. Our community has low-, moderate-, and high-impact approaches that meet you where you are and aspire to be as a performing artist.

You may ask yourself, "Why do I need to do this for 14 days?" BECAUSE you'll begin to:

1. Build Consistency and Discipline

This repetition exercise instills routine. By repeating this workout daily, you'll cultivate a dependable practice habit that mirrors the consistency needed for performance schedules and show runs.

2. Deepen Mind-Body Awareness

Familiarity with the workout allows performers to notice subtle changes — how their body and voice respond to stress, fatigue, hydration, and emotions. This awareness is vital for self-regulation and performance sustainability.

3. Improve Technique Through Muscle Memory

Repeating a movement or vocal drill allows the neuromuscular system to embrace the technique more efficiently. Over 14 days, movements become sharper, placement becomes more reliable, and support becomes more instinctual.

4. Create a Safe Container for Risk-Taking

When the structure is familiar, the artist can focus on nuance, breath, emotion, or new dynamics without needing to "learn" the new shapes or steps every time. This repetition permits *playing inside the form*.

5. Reveal Patterns and Plateaus

Doing the same thing for 14 days makes it easier to track progress or pinpoint where the body or voice may be compensating or stuck. This insight informs what needs to be added or shifted in the next training phase.

Resource Index

Wherever you are in your journey, access to the right resources can make all the difference. This is my curated list of the sources within the performing arts on colleges, conservatories, unions, grants, scholarships, housing tools, and NYC living resources. This resource list will be updated as more sources are found. Make it your goal to check monthly on *Fearless Perspectives* on Blog on LaquetSharnellPringle.com for updates!

Let this section be your library of launching pads. Return to it anytime you need fresh direction or new opportunities. The more informed you are, the more empowered you become.

As you look at the current resource list, you'll notice that Pages 31, 51, 97, 102, 110 use "**iamfearless**" to access fearless tools.

Page 13
- *Professional Theater Seating Capacity* — playbill.com/broadway-theatres

Page 14
- *Shubert Organization* — shubert.nyc
- *Nederlander Organization* — nederlander.com/about-us
- *Jujamcyn Theaters* — jujamcyn.com

Page 15
- *Lincoln Center* — lct.org
- *New York City Opera* — nycopera.com
- *New York City Ballet* — nycballet.com
- *American Ballet Theatre* — abt.org
- *The Metropolitan Opera* — metopera.org
- *Second Stage Theater* — 2st.com
- *Circle in the Square* — circlesquare.org
- *Hudson Theatre* — thehudsonbroadway.com
- *Lyric Theatre* — lyricbroadway.com
- *The Broadway League* — broadwayleague.com

Page 17
- *The Public Theater* — publictheater.org
- *Roundabout Theatre Company* — roundabouttheatre.org
- *Signature Theatre* — signaturetheatre.org
- *NYU Skirball Center* — nyuskirball.org

Pages 18 & 45
- *The PIT Comedy Theater* — thepit-nyc.com
- *Upright Citizens Brigade* — ucbcomedy.com/nyc

Page 18
- *WP Theater* — wptheater.org
- *Transport Group* — transportgroup.org
- *Freestyle Love Supreme* — freestylelovesupreme.com
- *Off-Broadway Theatre Guide* — playbill.com/article/how-to-tell-broadway-from-off-broadway-from-com-110450

Page 29
- *Sara Bareilles Biography* — britannica.com/biography/Sara-Bareilles

Page 30
- *Michael R. Jackson (NYU Tisch)* — tisch.nyu.edu/grad-musical-theatre-writing

Page 31
- *Lin-Manuel Miranda Biography* — britannica.com/biography/Lin-Manuel-Miranda

Page 33
- *Actors' Equity Association* — actorsequity.org
- *SAG-AFTRA* — sagaftra.org
- *American Guild of Musical Artists* — musicalartists.org
- *American Guild of Variety Artists* — agvausa.com

Page 35 & 110
- *Resume – LaQuet Sharnell Pringle* (included in book - use "**iamfearless**" to access fearless tools)

Page 36
- *Reel Today (Self-Tape Studio)* — reeltoday.com

Page 44
- *Broadway Sessions with Ben Cameron* — bencameron.nyc/sessions
- *Steps on Broadway* — stepsnyc.com/faculty/laquet-sharnell-pringle
- *Broadway Dance Center* — broadwaydancecenter.com/faculty/laquet-sharnell-

pringle
- *Peridance Center* — peridance.com

Page 51
- *Unavoidable Costs Chart* (included in book - use "**iamfearless**" to access fearless tools)

Page 63
- *Princess Grace Foundation* — pgfusa.org
- *American Theatre Wing / Jonathan Larson Grants* — americantheatrewing.org/grants
- *SAG-AFTRA Foundation Scholarship* — sagaftra.foundation
- *New York Foundation for the Arts (NYFA)* — nyfa.org
- *National YoungArts Foundation* — youngarts.org
- *The Entertainment Community Fund* — actorsfund.org

Page 65
- *Jacob's Pillow Scholarships* — jacobspillow.org
- *Dance/USA Fellowships to Artists* — danceusa.org
- *Theatre Communications Group (TCG)* — tcg.org

Page 81
- *Injury & Sleep Study* — pmc.ncbi.nlm.nih.gov/articles/PMC9960533
- *Broadway Cares / Equity Fights AIDS* — broadwaycares.org
- *R.Evolución Latina* — revolucionlatina.org

Page 82
- *Broadway Serves* — broadwayserves.org
- *Broadway Baby Mamas* — instagram.com/broadwaybabymamas
- *Broadway Babysitters* — broadwaybabysitters.com
- *The LGBT Community Center* — gaycenter.org

Page 85
- *Marti Gould Cummings* — marticummings.com
- *Katie Webber* — katiewebbernyc.com
- *Marla Louissaint* — marlalou.com

Page 96
- *Fractured Atlas* — fracturedatlas.org
- *NYFA Fiscal Sponsorship* — nyfa.org/fiscal-sponsorship

Page 97
• *Artists as a Startup Worksheet* (included in book - use "**iamfearless**" to access fearless tools)

Page 102
• *Legacy & Longevity Worksheet* (included in book)
• *Legacy Map & Reflections* (included in book)

Resume + Reel Templates

Your materials are often the first introduction someone has to your artistry. Whether applying to a conservatory, submitting for a showcase, or building a website, these templates will help you be polished, prepared, and confident.

Each template in this appendix is crafted with clarity, industry standards, and accessibility in mind, so you can focus less on formatting and more on telling your story with impact. Let your materials reflect the brilliance we already know you carry.

For access to the templates & videos within this book, visit the link below:
www.fyastudios.co/fearless-book-extras
password: iamfearless

Author

Face Card Photography

LaQuet Sharnell Pringle is the Founder of Fearless Young Artists Studios in Harlem, NYC. A Broadway veteran and educator, they champion diverse voices through original choreography, direction, and writing, and created The Onset Technique—grounded in Ease, Flow, and Connectivity—to help artists build sustainable careers and serve their communities.

www.ingramcontent.com/pod-product-compliance
Lightning Source LLC
Chambersburg PA
CBHW051545120626
46551CB00013B/1377